Franciscans
and
Creation

What is Our Responsibility?

Washington Theological Union
Symposium Papers
2003

Franciscans and Creation

What is Our Responsibility?

Washington Theological Union Symposium Papers 2003

Edited by

Elise Saggau, O.S.F.

The Franciscan Institute
St. Bonaventure University
St. Bonaventure, New York
2003

CFIT/ESC-OFM Series
Number 3

The articles in this book were originally presented
at a symposium sponsored by the Franciscan Center
at Washington Theological Union, Washington, DC,
May 23-25, 2003
This publication is the third in a series of documents
resulting from the work of the
Commission on the Franciscan Intellectual Tradition of the
English-speaking Conference of the
Order of Friars Minor.
(CFIT/ESC-OFM)

ISBN: 1-57659-190-5

Library of Congress Control Number
2003114678

Printed and bound in the United States of America

BookMasters, Inc.
Mansfield, Ohio

TABLE OF CONTENTS

Preface
Ilia Delio, O.S.F.   vii

Chapter One

Theology and Ecology in an Unfinished Universe
John F. Haught   1

Chapter Two

In the Household of our Sister, Mother:
A Practical, Franciscan, Ecofeminist Meditation
Gabriele Ühlein, O.S.F.   21

Chapter Three

A Call to Mutuality: Response to Ühlein
Dawn M. Nothwehr, O.S.F.   39

Chapter Four

Taking Nature Seriously: Nature Mysticism,
Environmental Advocacy and the
Franciscan Tradition
Keith Douglass Warner, O.F.M.   53

Chapter Five

A Franciscan View of Creation: Response to Warner
Franklin Fong, O.F.M.   83

Chapter Six

Is Creation a Window to the Divine?
A Bonaventurian Response
Zachary Hayes, O.F.M.   91

About the Authors   101

PREFACE

Creation is a vast and awesome mystery. From the furthest horizons of an ever-expanding universe to the organization of a single cell, every level of creation manifests intricate beauty. Francis of Assisi had tremendous love and respect for the non-human world of creation. Thomas of Celano writes how he would preach to flowers as if they were endowed with reason and pick up worms from the road so that they would not be crushed by the footsteps of passersby. Francis came to understand that all creation, like himself, is called to give praise and glory to God, and he identified with all creatures as a brother because he knew they shared with him the same beginning. Bonaventure, too, likened the diversity of creation to many stained-glass windows, each "window" of creation reflecting the power, wisdom and goodness of God. For Bonaventure, as for Francis, creation is a theophany, a manifestation of God's overflowing goodness reflected in the order, beauty and harmony of nature.

The notion of creation as the sacrament of God, which is integral to the Franciscan vision, has been lost in our present age, a loss which is noted on many levels. For those who are strict materialists, an evolutionary universe without purpose has given rise to a meaningless universe. Ecological disasters brought about by over-consumption and structures of domination continue to threaten the survival of the planet, and the stripping of ecosystems and natural habitats is affecting the survival of human life. On every level, violence continues to be inflicted on the world of God's goodness. In a confessional way, we must admit that the sacramentality of creation is being perversely violated by those intended to proclaim it, namely, human beings. Perhaps Bonaventure said it best. Sin has caused us to become blind and ignorant so that the book of creation, the first book by which we humans were meant to know and love God, has become illegible to us. Some people treat creation as a worthless book, trampling upon it and tearing it apart. Others think we can find God apart from the book of creation, and still others think the secrets of this book can be unlocked by the human mind so that we will come to know everything through this book, including (as Stephen Hawkings claims) the mind of God.

The new science today is offering glimpses into a strange yet awesome universe. More and more we find ourselves joined to creation at the hip. Because the Franciscan tradition affirms God's presence throughout creation, it has a vital role to play in realigning our relationship to creation. With its central incarnational focus, it can help raise awareness of our ecological responsibilities, which flow from our role as humans in the universe. The universe story, as Thomas Berry notes, is our religious story, and we must know this story if we desire the fullness of life.

This collection of papers is an effort to bring the tradition's theology of creation into dialogue with contemporary aspects of creation. We begin with John Haught of Georgetown University, whose evolutionary theology discloses a God of promise and hope, gently luring creation toward maximum beauty while allowing the complexities of nature to unfold. Gabriele Ühlein speaks of relationships in the household (*oikonomia*) of God's creation, highlighting Clare's contribution towards structures of equality and mutuality. Dawn Nothwehr discusses the need for mutual relationship as a moral stance toward creation. Keith Warner, a doctoral candidate in environmental science, highlights the reality of ecological disasters and the urgent need for Franciscan spiritual values of poverty, penance and mutual sustainability. Franklin Fong, a plant physiologist, testifies to the critical role conversion plays in our relationship to the environment. Throughout these papers we see that new structures of relationship to creation can come about only through new structures of consciousness—a consciousness integral to the spiritual journey and the fruit of ongoing conversion. Finally, Zachary Hayes offers the splendid Bonaventurian vision of creation as a window to the divine. His view complements that of Haught, both of whom describe the evolutionary universe as one endowed with meaning and purpose.

This is the third volume of symposium papers sponsored by the O.F.M. Commission on the Franciscan Intellectual Tradition (CFIT). We hope that what is offered here will catalyze further discussion and exploration. We who are bearers of the tradition firmly believe that the insights of our heritage have much to offer to the survival of our planet, which is in a perilous situation today. We are called to be in solidarity with every aspect of creation, realizing that creation is incomplete and yearns for its completion in God. We are heirs to a rich theological tradition that can provide a framework for incorporating environmental sensitivity into religious practice and activity. What is offered here is a step in this direction.

Ilia Delio, O.S.F.
Director of the Franciscan Center
Washington Theological Union

CHAPTER ONE

THEOLOGY AND ECOLOGY IN AN UNFINSHED UNIVERSE

John F. Haught

Holmes Rolston III, one of America's most renowned environmental ethicists, has written that because of human factors and failings

> . . . nature is more at peril than at any time in the last two and a half billion years. The sun will rise tomorrow, because it rose yesterday and the day before; but nature may no longer be there. Unless in the next millennium, indeed in the next century, we can regulate and control the escalating human devastation of our planet, we may face the end of nature as it has hitherto been known. Several billion years worth of creative toil, several million species of teeming life, have now been handed over to the care of this late-coming species in which mind has flowered and morals have emerged. Science has revealed to us this glorious natural history; and religion invites us to be stewards of it. That could be a glorious future story. But the sole moral and allegedly wise species has so far been able to do little more than use this science to convert whatever we can into resources for our own self-interested and escalating consumption, and we have done even that with great inequity between persons.[1]

Our species, Rolston and other environmentalists agree, is ruining the natural world. We humans are destroying rain forests, allowing the soil to erode, poisoning the air, and polluting rivers, lakes and oceans. We have created a dangerous greenhouse atmosphere and reduced the protective ozone layer. And we are daily destroying many irreplaceable living species. Common sense demands that we change our ways, but apparently we need much more than common sense to fire our ethical responsibility for the earth. What we need is a *vision*, one that can move us to a firm and permanent commitment to ecological responsibility within the context of natural flux and cosmic evolution.

Can Christian faith provide such a vision? And can theological reflection discover in tradition or scripture a groundwork for dedicated ecological action? It seems to me, speaking here as a Christian theologian, that this is one of theology's most important contemporary challenges, especially in view of well-known accusations that Christianity is itself in some way responsible for our environmental neglect. Such a serious indictment forces us to ask whether theology can demonstrate an *essential* connection between Christian faith and ecological concern. Can Christian faith provide truly motivating reasons for taking care of the nonhuman natural world?[2]

The Australian philosopher John Passmore, for one, doubts that it can. Belief in God and the "next world," he says, softens our sense of obligation to *this* world. Otherworldly piety even gives rise to an implicit hostility toward nature. The only substantial basis for environmental concern, therefore, is a radical naturalism, a belief system that sees nothing beyond the existence of the physical universe. According to Passmore, only if humans accept the fact that we are situated here on this planet in a universe barren of any transcendent governance, will we begin to take full responsibility for our terrestrial home.[3]

Passmore is right in characterizing much traditional Christianity as otherworldly to the point of neglecting the earth's well-being. His complaint is justifiable, given his understanding of what Christianity essentially is. Moreover, he compels us to acknowledge that Christian theology must do a much better job of displaying whatever ecological relevance it might have than it has done so far.

So, precisely how can Christian theology respond? It may begin by emphasizing that according to biblical faith the natural world is inherently good and that God has even become incarnate in the cosmos. It can point to exceptional exemplars of love of nature such as St. Francis, Hildegard of Bingen, Meister Eckhart, or Gerard Manley Hopkins. It must, in all candor, acknowledge that most of our saints, poets and theologians have had little formal concern about the well-being of nature. But at the same time, it may point to the fact that several distinct kinds of "ecological theology" are now emerging. For convenience's sake I shall call these 1) the *tradition-centered* (or "apologetic") approach, 2) the *sacramental* approach and 3) the *cosmic promise* approach. The latter weaves the biblical theme of promise into the new scientific awareness of a universe still in the making.

Each of these three proposals is insufficient when taken alone, but taken together they constitute a substantial beginning for a Christian ecological theology. Cumulatively they are capable not only of responding to accusations that Christian faith is indifferent to the welfare of nature, but they can provide the underpinning of a new vision of religiously inspired responsibility to the earth. Each of the three approaches relies on points made by the other, but adds its own emphasis. There is a good deal of overlap, but each has an accent not visible in the others. The three types are complementary in an additive sense: each is a piece of a whole puzzle.

As we shall see, the *cosmic promise* (or, more technically, the "cosmological-eschatological") approach becomes especially significant once we situate our reflections in the context of what science has demonstrated to be the *unfinished* condition of the physical universe. Cosmology has recently undergone a radical transformation, one that allows theology now to link up with ecological understanding in a way that would not have been available to our religious ancestors. Today it is imperative that theologians who address the contemporary ecological predicament attend very closely to what geology, evolutionary biology, genetics and especially scientific cosmology are telling us about the natural world. We shall find, I believe, that theological reflection on what science has shown to be a world still in the making can reconfigure the meaning of stewardship in an entirely fresh manner, one that may bring about a new appreciation of the close connection between biblical faith and our obligations to nature in process. But first let us see what we can say about Christian responsibility to nature even independently of any encounter with the world of contemporary natural science. (In this paper I shall limit myself to the world of Christian thought.)

1. A Tradition-centered (Apologetic) Approach

The first and probably the most familiar approach to ecological theology is one that finds in scripture and tradition adequate resources for a Christian response to the ecological predicament. We may call this approach "apologetic" because, as the Latin world *apologia* suggests, it "defends" biblical faith against the charge that it is ecologically hazardous or inconsequential. Examples of the apologetic approach include recent statements on environmental issues by the Pope, Catholic Bishops, the World Council of Churches and a growing number of theologians.[4] Their common message is that we have ignored the wealth of ecologically relevant material in the Bible and Christian tradition. Accordingly, what theology should be doing now is to retrieve this lost wisdom and allow it to address the present crisis. Theology will find numerous, often previously ignored, biblical passages and many other texts from the great teachers in the Church's history that proclaim the goodness and beauty of creation. It will come upon numerous ecologically relevant texts that it had barely noticed before we began recently to become aware of the fragility of life on this planet. How many of us, for example, have thought very much about the words in the Noah story in *Genesis*, where after the flood God made a covenant not only with human beings but with "every living creature"? And have we ever reflected on the profound significance the familiar words in Genesis 1:31 may have today: "And God looked at everything he had made, and he found it very good"?

The backbone of the "apologetic" approach, of course, is God's giving humans the task of "caring for" the garden in which they are situated (Gen. 2:15). Responsible stewardship, however, entails the practice of ecologically appropriate virtues: compassion, humility, moderation, detachment and gratitude. Since the immediate "causes" of our ecological crisis are commonly said to be human arrogance, greed, violence and the crude exercise of power, a renewed commitment to a biblically inspired ethic should lead directly to the repair of nature. Indeed, it is tempting to say that the solution to our ecological crisis lies simply in a serious return on the part of human beings to the practice of fundamental biblical values and classic religious virtues. Contrary to what critics of Christianity maintain, therefore, the apologetic approach insists that this tradition by no means lacks the basis for ecological conscientiousness. The fact is we have not attended to its ethical directives. Environmental abuse is not the fault of Christianity, as Passmore and other secular thinkers have argued. Rather, it is the result of our failure to take seriously the imperatives embedded in Christian faith.

What could be more fundamental in restoring our relationship to the natural world, for example, than earnestly practicing compassion? Would we be stretching Christian faith beyond its boundaries were we to extend its emphasis on sisterly and brotherly love toward all of creation? Is St. Francis's compassion toward animals or his discourse about brother sun and sister moon an unnecessarily revisionist straining of the meaning of love? For Christians, the paradigm of such widening of compassion for and deeper relationship to all of creation is revealed in the picture of Jesus as the Christ. The Gospels picture Jesus as one who constantly sought out deeper connections than those required by the customs of his time. They see him as passionately desirous of relating to those who were by all ordinary standards relationless: the sinners, the religiously despised, the sick and even the dead. Perhaps the central motif of his life was the embracing of what did not belong. Is it not conceivable then that the contemporary movement to include all of life and all of nature within the circle of our own compassionate care is a justifiable extension of the Spirit of Christ in our own time? An ecological theology may extend the circumference of Jesus' inclusive compassion for the unincluded to embrace the totality of nature.

Finally, there is an even more fundamental way in which theology may ground ecological concern in Christian tradition while at the same time defending itself (apologetically) against the claim that radical secularism or pure naturalism provides a more favorable climate for ecological solicitude than does theistic belief. Numerous classic texts of Christian tradition echo St. Augustine's oft-repeated observation that each of us is restless until we rest in God.[5] According to many religious traditions, in fact, we are each born with an insatiable desire for the infinite. From the Jewish, Christian and Islamic perspectives, only the inexhaustible mystery of God can ultimately satisfy us. But when the modern world formally abandoned the idea of God, it did not eliminate the infinity of our native longing. We remain *capax infiniti* (open to the infinite). Our unquenchable thirst for "more and more" stays with us as an anthropological constant. Having lost sight of its ultimate objective–the infinite God–this longing does not go away, but instead turns itself toward devouring our proximate environment, the planet we live on.

The restless human search for satisfaction is now engaged in the hollow project of squeezing the infinite out of what is increasingly exposing itself as utterly finite. Our tiny planet is unable to deliver the boundlessness that renders the human heart forever restless. We have not found on the earth a transcendent plenitude proportionate to the abysmal emptiness of our hearts. Thus, many of the earth's resources are now being used up with disproportionate rapidity, all in the senseless enterprise of milking infinity from a conspicuously bounded resource. Logically speaking, then, the solution to our disastrous exploitation of the planetary environment is not to deny the existence of the infinite mystery of God, but in conformity with our great religious traditions, to direct our longing toward it once again.

Evaluation of the Tradition-centered Approach

Over the past fifteen years or so, I have witnessed at close hand the emergence of ecological theology, and I would say that most theologians, along with many other Christians, have made the tradition-centered or apologetic approach the substantial core of their response to our present ecological situation. There is much to recommend this approach, and its retrieval of the tradition must surely be part of any adequate ecological theology today. However, I fear that it does not adequately address all dimensions of the current situation. On the positive side, it has made us read the Bible and traditional theology with new eyes and helped us peer more deeply into the ethical significance of the venerable teachings about creation, incarnation, divine wisdom, etc. But, as I shall argue below, it needs to be supplemented by the "sacramental" and "cosmic promise" approaches.

Before taking up the alternatives, however, I should first emphasize that the "apologetic" stance is entirely justified in opposing the simplistic allegations made by Passmore, Lynn White, Jr. and others that Christianity is the main cause of our environmental ills. The fact is that the secularist and scientistic assumptions of modern intellectual culture have led to a radical desacralizing of nature that in turn has permitted us to treat the earth as though it were merely instrumentally good rather than a value in itself.[6] In addition, the modern secularist outlook has generated a materialist philosophy of nature according to which life is reducible to lifeless chemicals and in which insensate "matter" is elevated to the status of ultimate reality.[7]

It is hard to imagine how such a picture of things could ever lead people toward the reverencing of nature that ecological ethics now requires. Barry Commoner points out that if we consistently followed the materialist creed that life is reducible to lifeless matter *in principle*, sooner or later this reduction will take place *in fact* as well.[8] Moreover, as Hermann Daly and John Cobb have shown at length, the causes of nature's present distress include run-away industrialization and naive economic assumptions about the unlimited resourcefulness of the earth, both of which are rooted in the materialist assumptions of modernity.[9] Christians, like others, bear much of the blame, but Christianity's and other religions' antimaterialism is inherently a restraining influence, and their cultivation of virtues of moderation and humility, were we to take them seriously, would lead us to accept our finitude and temper our will to exploit and destroy the natural world.

However, after acknowledging all of this, there is room to doubt whether it is enough for Christian ecological theology simply to restore the most familiar elements of the tradition. I strongly suspect that the present crisis calls for something more from theology than simply pointing us to relevant and often forgotten texts and teachings. Today we may need a more animating and far-reaching articulation of what it means to be Christian in an ecological age. In view of the unprecedented modern and contemporary devastation of nature, perhaps we should not place too protective a shield around our traditions, but instead allow them also to be creatively transformed, as indeed nature itself is being transformed in its own evolution. Religious faith, after all, springs to life most floridly during those periods of history when it faces radically new challenges. Can we be certain that Christian tradition in its purely classical formulations is fully adequate to the dimensions of the current environmental crisis? Is it perhaps conceivable that faith and theology are now being summoned by radically new circumstances, and especially by developments in scientific cosmology, to undergo a more sweeping metamorphosis than the apologetic approach alone would permit?

There seems to me to be something utterly interruptive about our current ecological situation, and so our religions are now being challenged to a much more thoroughgoing self-renewal than an exclusively apologetic approach would allow. For Christianity, as for all other traditions, innovative responses may be needed. Consequently, I shall now outline two alternative routes–not completely separable from each other or from our first approach–that theology may take in our time as it looks toward the future of humanity's relationship with the natural world.

2. The Sacramental Approach

For Christians the theological resources for an ecological renewal of faith can be found not only in biblical texts and doctrinal tradition, but also, and no less fundamentally, in the "sacramental" character of nature itself. To say that nature is sacramental simply means that, even apart from biblical revelation, nature in all of its beauty and diversity reveals the divine mystery–not just to Christians, of course, but to people of many traditions. A sacrament is anything through which we are gifted with a sense of the sacred; and it is especially nature's beauty and vitality that have communicated to humans an impression of the divine. In fact, it takes only a moment's reflection to realize that we really could not say very much about God at all apart from the richness and variety present in nature. Nature's sunlight, oceanic depths, fresh air, water, storms, rocks, trees, soil, growth, fertility, life, abundance, power, just to name several obvious examples, are perennially essential to religious metaphor. Even apart from traditional religious texts, therefore, nature's sacramental character gives us a deeply religious reason for taking care of it.

By acknowledging nature's inherent transparency to the divine, sacramentalism keeps us from turning our world into nothing more than raw material for our own human projects. Its sacramental capacity, therefore, should shield nature from diminishment at our hands. Without pantheistically identifying nature with God, as some traditionalists fear, the sacramental approach sees that the natural world is at heart a symbolic disclosure of God.[10] This gives nature a "sacral" quality that should divert our manipulative tendencies. And today, after Darwin and Einstein, we are in a position to envisage all natural sacraments as embedded in an even more encompassing sacrament, that of an entire evolving universe gradually revealing the divine to us in a dramatic way that previous theological ages could never have imagined. For ecological theology not to notice and profit from this magnificent revelation would be a most appalling oversight.

Sacramental ecology argues that apologetics, with its emphasis on classic texts, is not enough to ground an ethically motivating ecological theology. If we want a theology capable of responding to the full dimensions of the ecological crisis we must learn once more to revere the natural world itself for showing forth to us the sacred reality that underlies it.[11] And as I shall argue below, we cannot do this without the help of contemporary science and cosmology. Our spirituality has become so acosmic, so obsessed with themes of history and human freedom, so concerned with interpreting written texts, that it has lost touch with the sacramentality of nature. It is now time to resacramentalize theology.

For Christians this means especially that they place fresh emphasis on the biblical theme of creation. Western religious tradition has unnecessarily subordinated creation–and by implication sacramentalism–to the theme of redemption.[12] An exclusive emphasis on redemption has led Christian theology to exaggerate the "fallenness" not only of ourselves but also of the natural world. The assumption has been that redemption would be a momentous event only in proportion to the abysmal depths of a primordial Fall. By over-emphasizing the fallenness of both humanity and nature "in the beginning," nature has been made at times to seem perverse and therefore undeserving of our care. By exaggerating the fallenness of nature we have too easily lost sight of the original goodness of the entire creation that God declared to be "good." At the same time, an undue focus on the human need for redemption from evil has distracted us from the travail of the entire creation that, in St. Paul's words, also "groans" for radical renewal (Rom. 8:22). The renewal of nature to which Christian faith alludes need not be postponed until the "last day," but it can begin to become a reality here and now—no less so than the renewal of our personal lives can begin in the present.

The sacramental approach emphasizes the present renewal of nature when it interprets "sin" to mean more than just our human separation from God or from each other. Sin also signifies the current alienation of nature from humanity, its estrangement from God and from its own creative possibilities envisaged by God from the outset of creation. Accordingly "redemption" and "reconciliation" must mean not only the restoring of the divine-human relationship, but also the healing of the entire earth-community and indeed the renewal of the whole creation, beginning right now. The redemption of nature no more has to be delayed to the "end of time" than does the new creation of our own personal lives.

Likewise, for a sacramental-ecological theology, the redeeming "Christ" is no longer exclusively a personal, historical savior but, even more fundamentally, a cosmic presence—indeed the rejuvenating heart of an entire universe—as represented in the writings of Paul, John, Irenaeus and Teilhard de Chardin. We may even say that the whole cosmos is in some sense the "body of Christ." Concentrated and epitomized in the flesh and blood of Christ, the entire evolution of the universe becomes the corporeal expression of the very being of God.

A sacramentally shaped ecological vision also gives a cosmic dimensionality to eucharistic celebration. Eucharist symbolizes the healing not only of damaged human relationships but of our broken connection with the natural world as well. At the same time, a sacramental ecology gives fresh relevance to the doctrine of the Holy Spirit, the creative power that the Psalmist implores God to "pour out" so as to "renew the face of the earth."

This sacramental face-lift of theology calls in turn for new directions in Christian spirituality. It encourages, for example, a wholesome new sense of our intricate relationship to the natural world. In the past, the spiritual sensitivities of Christians have often been shaped by an anti-incarnational dualism that separates spirit from matter and thus distances us humans from nature. This dualism suppresses our natural intuition of being connected to an incalculably rich cosmic diversity and to a bodily existence completely continuous with the rest of the story of life on earth. The same dualism, incidentally, has also undergirded patriarchal exclusivism with its sinful oppression of women.[13] Sacramentalism, in alliance with prophetic themes of biblical faith, links respect for the earth very closely to the social and religious liberation of women; and it argues that our religious institutions will not seriously accept ecological responsibility until they have begun to treat women with justice, both socially and ecclesially.

The sacramental approach is typically allied with a sense of the interrelationship of all forms of life. For this reason a renewed sacramental realization of the intricate way in which human life is woven into the natural world should lead us to see how inseparable ecological concern is from the demands of economic justice. Much of our mistreatment of this planet's life-systems, after all, stems from the inequitable way in which the world's goods are distributed from region to region, or from nation to nation. Impoverished places on earth are often the most ecologically spoiled simply because their inhabitants must strip them bare for the sake of mere subsistence. Hence we cannot hope to restore the ecological integrity of such locales without also addressing the extreme poverty that exists there. At the same time, those of us who live in areas of material bounty and wealth must realize that our own extravagant use of the world's resources contributes disproportionately to the global perpetuation of ecological disarray. The Christian tradition is powerfully relevant and often effective on issues of social justice, but social justice must now become allied closely–and everywhere–with a more sacramentally oriented focus on *eco-justice*.

Evaluation of the Sacramental Approach

Along with the tradition-centered approach, a sacramental vision adds indispensable ingredients to the larger project of formulating an ecological theology. Today Christian theology in particular needs to retrieve a sacramental sense of the cosmos. Our ancient intuition of the revelatory character of the universe, now brought up to date by scientific cosmology, is perhaps the most significant theological and ecological contribution our second approach has to make. More explicitly than the traditional apologetics, a sacramental theology allows us to recognize the *intrinsic* relation between religious faith and contemporary ecological concern. It helps us to realize, for example, that without the freshness of air, the purity of water and the fertility of soil, the power of our most enduring symbols of God is diminished or lost. The integrity of nature is inseparable from the flourishing of religion. If we lose nature, as Thomas Berry puts it, we will also lose God.

Nevertheless, the sacramental approach is unable to give us a fully biblical or a distinctively Christian ecological theology. It can easily allow us to overlook the pivotal motif of biblical religion, namely, the theme of promise for the future.[14] In its justifiable longing to recapture the sense of our connectedness to the natural world, the sacramental approach does not always pay enough attention to the Bible's fundamental orientation toward *future* fulfillment. That is, it is often inclined to ignore what theology refers to as "eschatology," the biblical concern for future fulfillment. A biblically informed sense of what we may call "the *promise* of nature" must become central, I believe, to any explicitly Christian reflections on ecology. Moreover, when eschatology is conjoined with contemporary scientific cosmology, the theme of "nature as promise" can preserve the best of both the classical and sacramental contributions to ecological theology while extending them into fresh territory.

3. The "Cosmic Promise" Approach

Biblical scholars over the last century or so have gradually rediscovered eschatology as the core of biblical religion. Promise of future fulfillment is the central message of the Hebraic scriptures, of the teachings of Jesus, and it is the driving force of the Christian vision of the world.[15] But theology has also come to realize that eschatology–concern for future fulfillment–means not simply a hope for human survival in the "next world," but a conviction that *everything that happens* in the present world (or the present age) occurs within the context of a divine promise of future fulfillment.[16] Although "what happens in the world" has usually meant primarily the affairs of human history, neither the doctrine of creation nor contemporary scientific cosmology permits us to leave the natural world out of the compass of Christian hope. An integral theology, one attuned to the biblical spirit of promise as well as to astrophysics, geology, evolutionary biology and ecology, demands that we now view the entire universe, from its earliest beginnings to whatever end awaits it, as sharing in the same promise that the evangelist Luke, for example, beheld in the events associated with the birth of the Messiah.

An expansive and inclusive eschatological faith is convinced that the same divine promise that brought Israel and the Church into being has in fact always encompassed the totality of the cosmos. Eschatology, in its deepest and widest meaning, therefore, implies that a resplendent fulfillment awaits the *entire universe*. The divine promise first announced to Abraham pertains not only to the "people of God" but also, if we listen attentively to St. Paul in Romans 8:22, to the "whole of creation."

However, the question immediately arises as to whether
Christianity's eschatological orientation is ecologically helpful. Doesn't
future expectation actually uproot us from nature instead of reconcil-
ing us to it? Some ecologists fear that religious concern for a future fulfillment will allow us to tolerate ecological indifference in the present.
Hope for a future new creation, the argument goes, causes us to dream
so extravagantly of the age to come that we will lose interest in this one
and even let it slip toward catastrophe. We cannot ignore this concern.
After all, some kinds of biblical expectation, if taken in isolation, are
ecologically dangerous. For example, apocalyptic visions, when interpreted too literally and independently of other biblical forms of antici-
pation, may even take consolation in the prospect of this world's immi-
nent dissolution. Additionally, those individualistic earth-despising
brands of supernaturalist optimism–more a heritage of the Greek than
the biblical world–which seek an acosmic "spiritual" world as our final
destiny, seem to consign our present natural abode to final insignifi-
cance. Certain versions of eschatological fervor, in other words, do indeed appear to be ecologically problematic whenever they make "this
world" only instrumental to the human religious journey.

Secular environmental ethicists characteristically charge that
Christianity's futurist preoccupations make it inescapably indifferent
to the present well-being of the nonhuman natural world. Western religious doctrine and spirituality appear so otherworldly that the conservation of this world cannot easily become a priority for believers. Christianity, after all, has often taught that "we have here no lasting home"
and that our true abode lies elsewhere. But ecological responsibility
demands that we think of the earth, and the entire cosmos for that matter, as our *home*.[17] If we are going to have any lasting incentive to save
the beauties of creation, we need to feel deeply that we belong to nature
here and now. Much of the enthusiasm that ecological ethicists now
have for native peoples and non-Christian religions can be explained
by the impression that alternative faith systems seem to nest us more
comfortably within nature than do the dominant Western religious traditions. In the religions of many indigenous groups, for example, nature and humanity together formed a much more organic unity than
they do in the classic Christian view of the world. Primary religions,
generally speaking, do not seek to separate humans from nature. Perhaps, then, the emergence of eschatology in religious history is more of
a problem than a solution to the ecological question.

Biblical eschatology, in fact, seems to partake of a general religious restlessness that emerged in several places around the world in the first millennium BCE. During a historical period that philosopher Karl Jaspers has called the Axial Age, Indian mystics and Greek philosophers at times began to portray human destiny in terms of a withdrawal from "this world." Plato, for example, interpreted the natural world "here below" as a pale reflection of an ideal world that exists beyond time. The goal of our lives, from this perspective, is to find our way out of temporal existence into an eternity beyond time. Thus a sense of "cosmic homelessness" drifted into Western religion, and it became easier for us ever since to think of ourselves as strangers to nature. Christian spirituality has inherited much of this sense of cosmic homelessness; and so for that reason its eschatology often gives the impression of contradicting the ecological requirement that we experience ourselves as belonging to the wider world of nature.

How, then, is an ecological theology to address this troubling impression? It is undeniable, after all, that many influential religious teachings instruct us that excessive attachment to things, or to "this present age," or to natural objects does tie us down, enchaining and enslaving the human spirit. Moreover, Jews, Christians and Muslims view the restless, wandering figure of Abraham as a model of the deeply religious calling to leave the narrowness of "home" in pursuit of deeper fulfillment. In heeding the call to religious life, it seems that we are encouraged to pursue a life of detachment. Christianity, following ancient biblical patterns of thought, sees our life here on earth as an exodus journey, a pilgrimage, a desert wandering. In the New Testament, Jesus, the "Son of Man," is portrayed as having "no place to lay his head," and in Luke's Gospel he calls his followers to set their eyes on Jerusalem and not to look back toward what they have left behind. The Kingdom is more important than home and family.

If we turn to the East, we notice that the Buddha also has to leave home, to cease clinging to things and even to family, so as to find "enlightenment." And in Hinduism, the *sannyasin* finally forsakes home and family also, wandering to the edge of a forest or some other remote spot, so as to get closer to God. A great deal of the world's religious instruction, especially since the Axial Age, persuades us to accept the fundamentally homeless character of our existence as a condition of redemptive liberation. Accepting this homelessness is apparently essential to the religious adventure. But how do we reconcile religious pilgrimage with the ecological imperative to implant ourselves more deeply than ever in the earth? Can we practice "religious homelessness," in other words, without turning it into an ecologically ominous "cosmic homelessness"?

After some reflection on this question, I have come to the tentative conclusion that it is not the ideal of religious homelessness *per se* that is problematic. Rather it is our careless and unnecessary translation of religious into *cosmic* homelessness. The former, I propose, does not inevitably entail the latter. The endorsement of cosmic homelessness twists the ideal of religious homelessness into an escapism that makes nature a victim of our religious restlessness. Earth, for example, comes to be seen as a place to get *away from* in order to find salvation. The natural world becomes little more than a "vale of soul-making" in which to prove ourselves worthy of eternal life in some extra-cosmic domain. But if we love nature, how can we keep this affection from slipping toward a pure naturalism that enchains our spirits and frustrates our search for the ultimate liberation that faith promises? Can we ever truly learn to love God without turning our backs on earth? Can we come to cherish the natural world without surrendering our longing for the beyond? These are questions, perhaps the main questions, to which a Christian theology of nature must now attend.

I believe that we must admit in all candor that the religious formation that many if not most Christians have received has led them to harbor a deep suspicion that the human species does not essentially belong to nature or to the earth; and so in the name of religious aspiration they sometimes still hold themselves at a distance from nature. Many fear that it would be a capitulation to paganism, pantheism or romantic naturalism if they allowed the roots of their being to penetrate very far into the terrestrial soil. Unhappily, modern theology has done little to prevent the divorce from nature. Especially in the modern period, it has handed over the natural world to science and left to itself the task of interpreting classic religious texts, personal life and human history. It has left questions about nature and its future out of the field of theological interest. The majority of theologians still have little formal interest in the welfare of the nonhuman natural world.

However, I should hasten to add that it is not only religion and theology that have made us feel that we do not really belong to the cosmos. The so-called modern "scientific world-view" has also left us with the strong impression that we humans are essentially exiles from nature. In recent centuries much scientific thought has come to see nature as lifeless and mindless "stuff." As a result modern intellectual life has often assumed a materialist and pessimistic philosophy that gives the status of reality primarily to dead matter and views life and human consciousness as ephemeral accidents. Thus, in an essentially lifeless and spiritless world, it is not surprising that the human spirit can hardly feel at home.

Together, scientific materialism and religious dualism have perpetuated the ancient Gnostic idea that we are "lost in the cosmos." Can we, therefore, find a way to reconcile the religious requirement of living homelessly on the one hand with the ecological imperative to make nature our home on the other. We are torn–or so it would seem–between two appealing but apparently conflicting persuasions. We are drawn spiritually to the religious ideal of living without clinging to things that will diminish us and ultimately disappoint us. A spiritual homelessness is essential to the religious adventure even if physically we are tied to nature; and spiritual detachment can make us reluctant to see nature itself as an ethical concern. But, at the same time, many of us are now attracted to the ecological sentiment that the natural world has values worth preserving, that it is indeed our home.

How do we hold these two propensities together? Fortunately, and perhaps ironically, recent developments in natural science can come to our aid here. Careful reflection on the implications of contemporary scientific cosmology may allow us to belong to nature while at the same time letting us also pursue the life of religious detachment. Only a little knowledge of what science now teaches us about the universe can help us spiritually and intellectually to link our religious journey of homelessness to the ecological requirement of remaining friendly with and even firmly fixed to nature. We can now reasonably claim, in other words, that religious homelessness may exist harmoniously with a sense of our being quite at home in the cosmos. The following is an attempt to say why this solution is plausible.

The Cosmos in via

Over the last century and a half, science has demonstrated that the natural world itself is a restless adventure. No previous age has ever known–at least with the assuredness that we now possess–that the natural world is on a pilgrimage of its own. Our religions, including Christianity, had emerged long before science discovered that nature is itself a historical process and not something fixed or static. Today scientists realize that the physical universe is not changeless, eternal or necessary, as they formerly may have thought it to be. Although many people still do not believe it, the cosmos is most certainly a process, an evolution, an ongoing story. Humans live, in other words, in a universe that is still being created. The cosmos is not a stationary set of things frozen in essentially the same plodding status from all eternity, but an unfinished adventure open to what is perpetually new.

The famous Jesuit geologist and paleontologist, Teilhard de Chardin (1881-1955), has probably done more than any other Christian thinker to demonstrate how we can remain fully a part of the earth and the cosmos while also embarking on a momentous religious journey–along with the universe, not apart from it. Although, like others in his day, Teilhard was not fully aware of the scale of ecological degradation that modernity had unleashed, he developed a deeply incarnational and hopeful spirituality that can now frame our own efforts to construct an ecological theology. He did this by reinterpreting Christian faith in the context of cosmic and biological evolution.[18]

What evolution implies first and foremost is that creation is not yet finished. It is *in via*, on the way. The cosmos itself is essentially a pilgrimage. Hence, for us to embrace *this* universe we must align our own human existence with its inherent restlessness. Biology, geology and astrophysics now converge in challenging the ancient assumption that the universe is eternal and essentially unchanging. Taking seriously the new scientific picture of the world allows–even requires–that we embed our own unsettled lives within the much larger context of a *cosmic* restlessness. Only by accepting the universe's own homelessness, in other words, can we be at home in nature. Billions of years before we humans came along in evolution, the universe had already been on the move. During the past century and a half, science has filled out in remarkable detail the various episodes of this immense journey. I believe that there are implications for an ecological theology in these new accounts of the cosmic adventure.

At first glance, of course, one may wonder just what ecological-theological significance could possibly be squeezed out of the initially disturbing news that the cosmos itself is not at rest. According to the Big Bang theory, which almost all scientists accept today, the universe has a finite evolutionary past and an irreversible temporal trajectory. For all we know, therefore, our Big-Bang cosmos may presently be only in the early stages of a creative process that will last for many more billions of years. It is now clear that the universe is a still unfolding story.

But what does this mean for our own question about the relation-ship of ecology to theology? It means, fundamentally, that it is not only the human spirit that has undertaken an immense journey (especially through its religious wanderings) but that the entire cosmos is partner and prologue to our own homeless religious passage. Therefore, we do not need to abandon the natural world in order to follow the spiritual counsel to live homelessly. Indeed, we may even be permitted to say that our religious restlessness is a blossoming forth of the universe's own ageless adventuring. Our human hunger for transcendence is a conscious development of a general leaning toward the open future that has always been a hidden feature of the physical universe. Our religious striving toward the infinite is to be satisfied only by our attun-ing ourselves to the larger and longer cosmic odyssey into the future, not by extricating ourselves from it. The new scientific cosmology al-lows us to belong to the universe without our having to sacrifice the ideal of religious sojourning. Eschatology can embrace cosmology–"Your promise, O Lord, is as wide as the heavens" (Psalm 138:2).

So our religious homelessness does not have to be turned into cos-mic homelessness after all. Theologically viewed, we may now say that the universe—at its very core—is inseparable from promise. And so, we may learn to revere the natural world not simply because faith sees it as sacramentally transparent to God, but even more because it carries in its present perishable nature the seeds of a final, glorious future flow-ering. This means, in turn, that our current abuse of nature is not only a violation of nature's sacramentality; it is also a turning away from the promise that lies embedded in God's creation. In a properly biblical framework, then, our ecological recklessness is not just disobedience to our mission of stewardship, nor simply a sacrilege in violation of nature's sacramentality. It is fundamentally an expression of despair, of the dis-trust that the Bible considers to lie at the base of human sinfulness.

This promissory way of looking at nature requires that we give a fresh understanding to the notion of stewardship. Stewardship, in the framework of a cosmology framed by the theme of promise, must amount to much more than conservation. Conservation is essential, of course. We need to appreciate the many millions of years of evolution-ary striving and achievement that produced the ecological richness that preceded human emergence. It goes without saying that there is an in-trinsic worth in earth's biosphere that deserves our best efforts at preser-vation. But perhaps the most fundamentally Christian reason to

participate in the saving of living diversity is that nature is always preg-
nant with the promise of humanly incalculable future outcomes. We do
not have access to the Creator's vision of the cosmic future, but we may
confidently believe that every present contains the promise of future
fulfillment.[19] A Christian vision will lead us to strive not to get out of
the world but to do what we can to shepherd this still unfinished universe toward the fulfillment of the promise that underlies and impels it
toward the future.[20]

Endnotes

[1]Holmes Rolston, III, "Science, Religion, and the Future," in Mark Richardson and
Wesley Wildman, eds., *Religion and Science: History, Method, Dialogue* (New York and London: Routledge, 1996), 79.

[2]For a fuller development of the present essay, see my book, *The Promise of Nature*
(Mahwah: Paulist Press, 1993).

[3]John Passmore, *Man's Responsibility for Nature* (New York: Scribner, 1974), 184.

[4]John Paul II, "Peace with God the Creator, Peace with All of Creation" (World Day
of Peace Message, Jan. 1, 1990); John Paul II, *The Ecological Crisis: A Common Responsibility*,
nos. 1, 15, December 8, 1989; *Renewing the Earth* (1991); Drew Christiansen, S.J., and Walter
Grazer, eds., *"And God Saw That It Was Good"* (Washington, DC: United States Catholic
Conference, 1996); The American Conference of Catholic Bishops, "The Columbia River
Watershed: Caring for Creation and the Common Good" (February, 2001). Documents
and discussion of some of the earliest work on ecological issues by the World Council of
Churches may be found in Charles Birch, William Eakin and Jay B. McDaniel, eds., *Liber-
ating Life: Contemporary Approaches to Ecological Theology* (Maryknoll, NY: Orbis Books,
1990).

[5]Augustine of Hippo, *The Confessions of St. Augustine* (Garden City, NY: Image Books,
1960), 44.

[6]This point is persuasively argued by Rupert Sheldrake in *The Rebirth of Nature: The
Greening of Science and God* (New York: Bantam Books, 1991), 9-96.

[7]For a thorough discussion of the implications of materialist philosophical assumptions (based on the "fallacy of misplaced concreteness") for both economics and our treatment of the natural world, see Herman E. Daly and John B. Cobb, Jr., *For the Common Good*
(Boston: Beacon Press, 1989), 25-110. See also my book *The Promise of Nature*, 11-38.

[8]Barry Commoner, "In Defense of Biology," in Ronald Munson, ed., *Man and Nature*
(New York: Dell Publishing Co., 1971), 44.

[9]For support of this claim, once again, I recommend a close reading of Daly and
Cobb's book, *For the Common Good*.

[10]See Michael J. Himes, O.F.M. and Kenneth R. Himes, O.F. M., "The Sacrament of
Creation," *Commonweal*, 117 (Jan. 12, 1990): 45.

[11]See Thomas Berry, *The Dream of the Earth* (San Francisco: Sierra Club Books, 1988).

[12]See Thomas Berry, *The Dream of the Earth*. See also Matthew Fox, *Original Blessing*
(Santa Fe, NM: Bear, 1983).

[13]Both Rupert Sheldrake and Thomas Berry have made this point respectively in
their books referred to above. See Sheldrake, 43, 56, 74f. and Berry, 138-162. They are both
indebted to Carolyn Merchant, *The Death of Nature* (San Francisco: Harper & Row, 1980).

[14]To readers unfamiliar with theological method, let me explain briefly why Christian theology cannot ignore the theme of promise, even when it is dealing with nature. Theology, as David Tracy has written, is systematic, critical reflection on the classics of a religious tradition. See *Blessed Rage for Order: The New Pluralism in Theology* (New York: Seabury Press, 1975). Among the classics of Christian tradition, of foremost importance is the Bible. In this vast and variegated body of sacred texts, the most fundamental and recurrent theme is that God is a maker and keeper of promises. Hence, for Christian theology to make the theme of promise optional, as both the apologetic and the sacramental approach tend at times to do, would be to abandon what is central to the tradition. By emphasizing the theme of the "promise of nature," I am attempting to take the biblical substance of Christian tradition much more seriously than other ecological theologies, especially that of Thomas Berry, have done.

[15]For support see the writings of Jürgen Moltmann, for example, *Theology of Hope,* trans. James Leitch (New York: Harper & Row, 1967) and *The Experiment Hope,* ed. and trans. M. Douglas Meeks (Philadelphia: Fortress Press, 1975).

[16]For an earlier development of points made in this section see my book *God After Darwin* (Boulder, CO: Westview Press, 2000), 159-164.

[17]As I will show later on, being fully at home in nature does not require that one adopt an exclusively sacramentalist approach.

[18]See especially Pierre Teilhard de Chardin, *Christianity and Evolution,* trans. Rene Hague (New York: Harcourt Brace & Co., 1969)

[19]For us to throw away our natural heritage would be equivalent to throwing away a promise. For this reason we may be glad that the American Catholic Bishops' pastoral, *Renewing the Earth,* has identified the virtue of hope as the fundamental posture of Christianity toward the ecological situation of our time.

[20]I do not have space here to consider the anticipated questions that arise from recent astrophysical scenarios of a universe that will sometime in the distant future no longer be able to sustain life. The eventual demise of the cosmos, however, does not vitiate the theme of nature's promise that I have been highlighting. To the Christian there should in principle be no more difficulty trusting that the whole universe-story will be taken redemptively into God's life than there is in trusting that we ourselves will be saved by God's compassionate care. For now I must be content to affirm that it is no longer theologically or cosmologically conceivable that human destiny could ever be separated from cosmic destiny and vice-versa. If we dwell within the compass of God's promise, so also does the entire universe.

CHAPTER TWO

IN THE HOUSEHOLD OF OUR
SISTER, MOTHER:
A PRACTICAL FRANCISCAN, ECOFEMINIST MEDITATION

Gabriele Ühlein, O.S.F.

Introduction: Daring an Ecofeminist Annunciation

A mid-western Passion Sunday morning: crisp, sunny and full of spring
promise. I am in the happy company of my sisters. I watch them ready-
ing for procession in the Motherhouse chapel. Mostly they are my el-
ders. Many are seated, too unsteady for walking now, having walked
already their goodly share. There are numerous other women and a
man, lay covenant members, standing ready to join the procession with
full voice. Present too, are the adult children of a woman, soon to be a
grandmother, who is in the process of applying for vowed membership
with us. Sun streams through the brilliant glass of our chapel windows,
and the colors illustrating Mary's *Magnificat* fall on to the shoulders of
my sisters who are distributing palm branches to one and all. The image in the lower left corner of the Clare *Tavola* comes to mind. It is Clare,
in the company of the women of her household, receiving a palm branch
from Bishop Guido. Is the gift of the palm a *transitus* annunciation? Is it
a signal to Clare that all is in readiness? That this will be the night the
Friars will meet her, torches ablaze, as she leaves one way of life behind
to begin another? And what of the palm branches today? What annunciation awaits us amid hosannas, as the Passion Sunday liturgy reminds
us of crucifixion?

In my own household, about twenty-five of my sisters have died in
the past three years. We have received one new candidate to our vowed
way of life, covenanted with some dozen lay members and are exploring consecrated widowhood as a potential new form of membership.
We are contemplating the building of a parking facility and new hospi-
tal on our land and count the cost in precious trees and green space. I
have sisters yearning for the day when we are no longer dependent for
the Eucharist upon a celebrant external to our community, while others
of us are scandalized by the presence of our sisters in the pulpit. I am

preparing for an international general chapter with women from numerous countries who oppose the war that our own country has declared. I shall sit in council with women who from one country are fac-
ing the diminishment of sickness and aging, and who from another country have the challenges of persecution, burgeoning youth and new beginnings. There will be women who have already feasted on the fruits
of refounding and renewal, as well as women who feel a call to the
preservation of form and tradition, albeit in a contemporary context.
As the words of the Passion Sunday Liturgy call me back to attention, I
feel the tension of a prevailing theology that, for privileged believers,
centralizes redemption in a crucifixion. And I feel encouragement from
the reading of a passion story that speaks, if only in its last stanzas, of
the fidelity of the women at the cross and the grave. For better or worse,
I am not spared the stretch.

    Much as her household experience in the company of the
Offreduccio women shaped Clare's gospel response, so do my sisters
form me in my own call, shaped as it is by the privileged, white, middle
class, professional status that my female Franciscan life in the United
States affords me. Before joining this community, I already knew the
price of patriarchy. Graduate study awakened my feminist awareness
and gave my experience a vocabulary. My Franciscan formation provided the necessary theological constructs to make the ecological connections. In, with and through my community, I come to speak in an
ecofeminist voice. In, with and through my Franciscan expression, I
experience the tensions typical of all women conscious of their place at
the margins. In my own community and in that of the broader American Franciscan Federation, these tensions are incarnate in four ways:

- in a painful sensitivity to long-standing patriarchy-sustaining thinking and methodology;
- in the more recent "renewal" evolution toward the centrality of
  personal experience;
- in the newly urgent emphasis on nature and body, and
- in the ever present difficult choices between the transformation of
  tradition and the revolution that new paths will require of us.

The feminist critique of patriarchy-sustaining thinking and methodology

    The basic initial concerns to which feminists of all stripes commonly
give voice are similar to the social and political inequities that date back

to the suffragettes of the Victorian period. These issues are usually politically direct—votes, jobs and education for women. Critique and action are based on the simple truth that was asserted by early Victorian feminists—*women are people too*! (and their voice ought to matter!) By the 1960s feminists also began to critique the underlying cultural stereotyping that made it difficult for women, even when financially secure, to opt for careers. Quickly feminists discovered that sexist roots extended beyond capitalism and economics to sociological and psychological constructions that are continually culturally reified. Indeed, cultural patriarchal values can be shown to reveal the "prototype" of social domination in all its forms.[1]

No wonder communal forms of organization and leadership in our own vowed life evolved so rapidly once their underlying motives were re-thought and re-imagined. Who of a particular vintage in the Franciscan Federation (and in so many other communities of religious women) has not lived through varieties of necessary experimentation with democratic forms and adult modes of responsibility. As we experiment with new ecologies of participation and membership, ever-new challenges confront community life. While no longer overtly patriarchal in most instances, habits of domination, especially in their more benevolent guises, require conscious and difficult inner work. Community continues to evolve. There is a willingness to struggle with appropriate open and closed sessions at meetings for vowed and non-vowed members. There is openness to team building and the discernment of leadership-election by considering teams. There is ongoing exploration of obedience and authority concerns, and there are circles of dialogue to support one another at times of systemic impasse. All these were unheard of just a generation or two ago, and we are still learning!

The more recent "renewal" evolution toward the centrality of personal experience

In my experience, whenever there is an attempt to define a Franciscan, no one description suffices. Defining a feminist requires equally multiple descriptors.[2] Feminists, both men and women, are aware that sexism is a multivalent form of culturally imbedded oppression. Most feminists agree that if "there is a universally dominated class, surely it is women."[3] The evidence is clear. "Public, formal and male-dominated activities almost always have more cultural respect than the domestic, less visible and more socially intimate activities of women."[4]

Feminism is concerned, then, with the abolition of those factors that aid and abet "the continued and systematic domination and subordination of women."[5] Within what began as the Women's Liberation Movement, the issues and concerns of feminists have continually broadened. This widening of concern is similarly reflected in what we might call in our community experience "the diversification of ministries." Feminist issues now focus on the inclusion of the separate and distinct voices of women in poverty, women in developing countries, women of color, to consider but a few. Cultural and methodological critique continues to inform the struggle. "Indeed, the increasing chorus of minority voices has been the single most important development in feminist work."[6]

I might also say that the increasing chorus of the "minority" voices among us is the single most important development in the evolution of our own communal ecologies. The Franciscan tradition has always valued *minores*, the voice of the youngest and the myriad ways in which individual sisters and brothers mirror no less than God. It has taken centuries and the *aggiornamento* of Vatican II to begin the embodiment of a mutual sensitivity to the whole *and* to the individual. This demonstrates the potency of the cultural press to orderly domination and product-oriented objectification. In a kind of corrective evolution of vowed community consciousness, the individual experiences of religious women began to be valued more highly by both peers and leadership alike. Public and highly regimented activities of a former time gave way to the pursuit of individual interior growth and development. Experiences diversified, and the skills needed for social intimacy and individual spiritual deepening were encouraged and introduced into formation programs. New concerns arose and continue to arise. New ways to be of service replace institutionalized expectations. Self-initiated ministries are multiplying. Given their own radical individual responses to the gospel call, our founders would be pleased, I think.

The newly urgent emphasis on nature and body

In the chorus of feminist voices, ecofeminism is a dynamic and evolving blend of feminism and ecological politics that addresses the objectification of women and of nature. Coined in 1972 by Françoise d'Eaubonne, the term *Ecologie-Féminisme* referred to the insight that the ecological compromising of the planet is the result of a desire for profit endemic to a male patriarchy. Ecofeminists were those that desired a world in which nature was "green again for all" and in which human beings were treated as people first and not marked as male or female.

Only women, she argued, could bring about such an ecological revolution.[7] While some might argue with that last sentence, d'Eaubonne's initial appreciation of the interaction of human oppression and environmental abuse sanctioned by a patriarchal worldview remains the primary perspective of contemporary ecofeminism.

The ecofeminist position holds that our present ecological disasters are a result of misguided sexist institutions and systems. They are sensitive to the often-unconscious association of women, bodies and nature and to how all three are devalued in a system of masculinist domination. Ecofeminists argue for the replacement of such practices as domination, destruction and exploitation. They suggest the implementation of alternative strategies that honor the unique contributions of each participant in the earth community. This view is contrary to the patriarchal dream of human omnipotence at the expense of women's ways, women's bodies and women's values (or more pointedly, nature's ways, nature's bodies and nature's values).

A clever shorthand for the ecofeminist view is *to insist that bodies do indeed matter.* Ecofeminists affirm that a truly human incarnation is a profound ecological project of respectful collaboration for the enhancement of no less than all the participants of the earth community. It is clearly evident that we now face an epoch in which the rise and fall not only of entire peoples but also of entire species depend on human dispensation. We understand now the sensitive ecological balance of our planet in ways undreamed of by most of our founders and most certainly by Francis and Clare. We can document the actual degradation of the environment–and know it as the price exacted for the cultural preferences of mind over matter, men over women, colonizers over indigenous populations, productivity over presence (here one can also read youth over age) and personal profit over communal vitality.

We can experience degradation in the ecology of our own religious community life (that is, the degradation of community relationships and responsibilities) via similar dichotomies. For example, we are inculturated to prefer what is spiritual over what is bodily and vigorous, youthful productivity over reflective and receptive presence. Thus many of us are ill-prepared for the diminishment that aging often brings. Nothing drives home the point that bodies matter more potently than when they no longer work in the manner to which we have become accustomed or when we find our community no longer able to sustain what we thought was essential to our way of life. We are not adequately prepared to understand that decrease and decline do not mean absence of blessing. Many of us, having tasted the short-term benefits of individualism, now have difficulty in finding a meaningful fidelity to the whole in a manner that does not compromise our newfound individual integrity. Likewise, having tasted various degrees of liberation from gender oppression, we struggle with "what is ours to do" as we interact with and are affected by oppressive systems.

The ever present difficult choices between the transformation of tradition and the revolution that new paths will require of us.

Fashioning a corrective for the old dichotomies of spirit over flesh, mind over matter, men over women and so on, raises particular identity issues for ecofeminists. Betty Roszak questions if it is good for women to be identified as close to nature.

> Do women have a special calling to save humanity and the Earth through a superior compassion and wisdom? Or is this just another repetition of the stereotyping we tried so hard to break? Are we not being used again subtly in the service of male power? By acknowledging a special relationship between women and nature, do we reinforce the projection of male responsibility onto women? . . . As feminists we need to guard as much against a new sentimentalized interpretation of woman as against the romanticization of nature. . . .We must be wary of setting ourselves apart as women in a new version of the Noble Savage who bears all wisdom and will redress the wrongs and injustices of the world.[8]

The point is well taken. Women's concern for Earth can indeed be co-opted by existing patriarchal assumptions. Care for Earth then, becomes *mere* women's work. While Betty Roszak draws gender lines in her analysis, other distinctions can be equally marginalizing. The same identity issues can be translated into my own Franciscan Third Order Regular experience. For example, do Franciscans have a special call to save humanity and care for Earth through our *Canticle* tradition? Is Earth care merely for the religious minority? On the other hand, have we romanticized our nature connection, making it more a spiritual kinship than an actual familial responsibility? Do we set up a we/they dichotomy and identify ourselves with those who feel a call to "green living"? Is it enough to dedicate some resources to the establishment of a justice/ecology office for those inclined to respond to such concerns and assume that we have done our communal part? Precisely because embodying an Earth connection challenges primary cultural dichotomies and asks of us far reaching life-changes, it is often easier to tolerate the marginalizing of those who minister in such ways and let their efforts absolve us from further participation in Earth justice work.

Relative to the marginalizing of women and others doing Earthwork, Ynestra King identifies three possible responses that can be of some use to us as we consider a Franciscan ecofeminist incarnation.[9] Her first suggestion is that women could abandon the connection with nature, which Sherry Ortner has identified as a source of perpetual devaluation in a patriarchal context.[10] This strategy relies on the acceptance of the prevailing culture's definition of what constitutes the highest value, sublimating all others towards its pursuit; and thus business can continue as usual. Simply put, this strategy accepts that farmers will always be of lower rank than corporate businessmen unless farmers become corporate businessmen too. In a Third Order Regular Franciscan ecology, similar ranking and marginalizing might have to do with the value placed on education, kinds of service, energy, kinds of living situations, etc. Certainly in our religious community life, we have, in the past, placed a high value on such things as obedience, productivity, uniformity, quantity, etc., and marginalized such things as questioning and evolution for the sake of preserving the presumed unchanging good of the institution. In its most virulent incarnation, this strategy presumed that laywomen "in the world" were of lower rank than religious who "left the world." In such a value system, ecofeminists working on behalf of women in the world and for the world would have had a very low standing indeed.

The second strategy in response to a devalued earth-connected feminine is to place a high value on women and their earth-connection without any reference to the masculine "other" at all.[11] This tactic serves to usurp dominant oppressive assumptions and to establish a separate gender-based preferential option for the feminine. There are many ways to do this and not just via Earth connection or gender distinctions. Divisions can be drawn and opposites polarized in any oppressive system. In short, "they" are not "us," and the concomitant behavior in a community ecology is familiar to most—one must opt out of oppressive constructs, not participate in their perpetuation, marginalize the oppressor as the oppressor marginalizes us. This strategy is likely when change comes too quickly or, as the case may be, not quickly enough. In my Franciscan experience, such a strategy profoundly affects liturgical cel-

ebrations and provincial gatherings, as well as other forms of communal participation. Boycott is powerful and can, over time, effectively
bring well-intentioned "business as usual to a standstill." It is the strategy of revolution.

The third way to address dualities, whether in regard to Earth-con-
nectedness, gender, theology, or any other arena, is to change entirely
the presupposed dualistic context that such polarization implies. For
example, when confronted with the devaluing of women because of an
identification with earth (mere matter), one can simply affirm the non-
optional nature of human earth-identification. This changes the context
entirely. If we are human, whether male or female, we are in, of and
through earth. This is the strategy of transformation. It relies on a fundamental shift in awareness and on a capacity to move from seeing
disparities and seemingly irreconcilable differences to a search for common ground. In a community ecology, a parallel realization is that we
are one *and* indeed many *at the same time.* Such a position calls for the
simultaneous validation of multiple perspectives within a larger con-
tainer of connection, and thus it is the least "logical" strategy. To be
successful, it will require the careful building of trust and the conscious
tending of the emotional field surrounding issues of "belonging." At its
best, such consciousness can allow for whole-hearted affirmation that,
for better or for worse, "we" are "they."

Belonging to the Household of our Sister, Mother

From the above descriptions we see that, just as ecofeminism must
grapple with appropriate modes of human participation in the earth
community, resonant experiences of grappling consciously with our own
participation in the ecology of community life abound. Of great comfort to me in this regard is the Franciscan *Canticle* tradition. When Francis
composed his hymn of praise, he probably did not have in mind the
care of the earth, as we think of it. It is a great grace that this hymn may
yet serve us in the context of our degraded Earth ecology. But more
than the proclamation of creaturely kinship is required. How we might
best incarnate that kinship is the driving question.

Since I have been making much of gender in this meditation, it seems
fitting that my attention turn to Clare, even as I speak of Francis's *Canticle.* Perhaps it is because of the opening Palm Sunday meditation or
perhaps because we are now in the seven hundred and fiftieth anniver-
sary year of her death that she is so present to me. In *Clare of Assisi,*
Ingrid Peterson makes much of the fact that Clare's spirituality was

nurtured among the women of the household into which she was born.[12] Indeed, it came to its full flowering among the sisters that God afforded her in the household at San Damiano. I think of Clare as embodying a kind of Franciscan feminism, daring possibilities that oppressive patriarchal structures consistently attempted to make over in their own image. I also think of Clare as consciously embodying a radically new household ecology: spare, generous, frugal, wise, egalitarian, all embracing and, with care and concern, flung as wide as her knowledge and experience allowed. I call to mind, too, the root of the word "ecology," that is *oikos* ("home") in Greek. Hence, ecology might literally be understood as the *oikos-logos*–"the truth of the home." Of course, I do not presume to think that Clare had ecofeminist strategies in mind as she revolutionized and transformed religious life options for women. Nonetheless, I propose that her "household" sensibilities can be a kind of archetype for contemporary Franciscan ecofeminist practice. I also do not presume to make such a practice an exact correspondence to Clare's San Damiano model. The *oikos-logos*–"the truth of the home" in the medieval Christian world of Clare's experience is vastly different from the *oikos-logos*–"the truth of the home" that humans experience today.

Making a "Deep Ecology" Connection

Perhaps the most different contemporary understanding of the "truth of the home" results from the realization that humans are potent co-participants in a vital web of life, the extent of which is not even today fully known. Deep ecologists begin with this fact. Arne Naess first used the term "deep ecology" in 1973,[13] intending to offer a corrective for the more "shallow" ecology that assumes the human to be the primary referent in the biosphere thereby giving them objective dominion over nature. According to deep ecologists, by limiting our sphere of concern to that of the human alone, we are guilty of an anthropocentric error that ultimately diminishes the very quality of life humans value. Ecofeminists and deep ecologists, then, have this in common: a recognition of the prevailing *anthropocentrism* (ecofeminists might more readily say *androcentrism*) at the root of the degradation of the natural world. A deep ecologist also presumes the human capable of a kind of spiritual transformation best understood as "ecological self-realization"– that is, the ability to extend self-identity beyond the human to include the non-human world. To practice deep ecology is to "cease to understand or see ourselves as isolated and narrowly competing egos."[14] In so doing, we commence a transformation that begins via an identification with other humans, then extends to other creatures, and ultimately to the biosphere as a whole.[15]

There is no possibility that Francis had deep ecology principles in mind when he ministered to the inhabitants of Gubbio, humans and wolf alike, or when he addressed himself to other creatures great and small. But there is no doubt that Francis experienced an inner transformation that can be likened to a kind of "ecological self-realization"–the ability to extend self-identity beyond the human to include the non-human world. By the end of his life, Francis understood that God had not only given him two-legged brothers, but also sisters and brothers it would take another mystic or "deep ecologist" to recognize today. Thus Francis, like Clare, can be a kind of prototype, modeling new kinship possibilities in the ecology of community.

On a more modest scale, the same kind of "ecological realization" occurs in community life when we become conscious enough to "cease to understand or see ourselves as isolated and narrowly competing egos." As a consequence, I am certain that the meditation on and the incarnation of hospitable and generous intentional community is the religious practice most suited to the dismantling of patriarchal structures and the healing of oppressive dichotomies. This is a very slow transformation process, fraught with trial and error. Yet, even as we struggle to integrate new human members who are different from those in the dominant group, we learn valuable connection-making skills that may yet allow us to aid well the likes of Sister Water herself.

Grounding our Theological Reflection

The trans-species familial sistering and brothering that earth's ecological degradation now requires of the human necessarily will call for a rethinking of all our relationships: human to human, nature to human, and most significantly, God to human. Perhaps it is best to take a cue from Francis, and to begin with God as he does:

Altissimo, onnipotente,	*Most High, all-powerful,*
bon Signore,	*good Lord,*
tue so le laude, la gloria,	*Yours are the praises, the glory,*
e l'onore et onne benedizione.	*the honor and all blessing.*

A te solo, Altissimo,	*To You alone, Most High,*
se confano,	*do they belong,*
e nullo omo è digno	*and no one is worthy*
te mentovare.	*to mention Your name.*
Laudato sie, mi Signore,	*Praised be You, my Lord,*
cun tutte le tue creature. . . .	*with all your creatures. . . .*

Francis clearly indicates that, from the beginning, all is for God, for divine praise. In all its diverse creativity, the creature world is for a kind of revelation that evokes no less than the awe and praise of the human that sees it, that experiences it. The *Canticle's* family of cosmic brothering and sistering is like an intentional community that has as its charism the revelation of God. The vocation of the cosmos is to evoke celebratory gratitude and divine praise. Given what we now know of the cosmic story, we can say that in the slow and gradual fullness of its evolution—every event, every creature, participates in this Godly purpose. Evolution is thus God-work and, ecologically speaking, is profoundly sensitive. What each creature becomes *matters*. This is so because each creature, by its very coming into being, impacts the environment for the next generation. Slowly, creature by creature, experience by experience, event by event, conditions arise that are exactly right for the next evolution. What each creature becomes matters. It is so because each creature in its becoming participates in the intention of God, from the beginning, to be with us. Thus, each creature, in its becoming, contributes something to the experience and revelation of nothing less than God. I like to think that this is what Francis intuits as he praises God through all the creatures and events he lists by name, even including Sister Death.

In both the smaller communal ecology that we have been considering and the more global Earth ecology, the same process of divine revelation is effectively present to an equal degree. This is what Clare intuits as she exhorts us to contemplate, to gaze and to see no less than Christ in one another. If even one of my sisters had not chosen our way of life, how different I might be, how different we would be, and how different she would be. This is an awesome thought. Likewise, in considering the events of my life, there is for me great mystery and no little awe in the manner in which doors open and close, opportunities arise and even illness and difficulties, considered in hindsight, have a seeming purpose. I can think of no clearer meditation to help me experience *mattering*, to help me experience the potency of incarnation. God intends to be known: through Christ, through my life, through my community. It is God's good will to be experienced, and, amazingly enough, we are entrusted with the details. If this is so in my community, how much more so in the community of Earth. I can think of no clearer meditation to confirm my Franciscan ecofeminist position as well.

Re-visioning a Canticle Conversion

It seems such a simple thing, to say that we are entrusted with the details. Yet, it is the details that matter. It matters that I am a woman. It matters that we are Franciscan. It matters that we are aging. It matters that we come together in ways that are familiar and in ways we have never experienced before. For the past three years, Third Order Regular women from a host of various congregations have been attending Franciscan Federation national workshops that stress the call to conversion that a *Canticle* consciousness asks of us today. Conditions are ripe for such earth-contexted conversations and not only in Franciscan circles. The Leadership Conference of Women Religious has chosen to focus on ecology at the 2003 annual meeting as well. It matters that ecological conversation is gradually becoming mainstream community conversation!

While the content of the Franciscan Federation's *Canticle of Conversion* program lays a careful cosmological foundation, the potency of the workshop is in its more experiential aspects. It is a way for diverse Franciscans to make conscious together how we are, in this earthly situation, sistered and brothered and to bring into awareness such past experiences for the sake of a sustainable future. While we may have often gathered to explore our Franciscan life, the Franciscan Federation has not called us together in such a clear ecological context before.

At these gatherings, we tell stories of finding God's blessings in creation, of personal responses to earth degradation and of the suffering that accompanies disregard for nature. We share how earth consciousness has evolved in our own lives and how we have come to a new eco-justice awareness in our ministries and in our day to day community life. In short, we share the details of how we are sistering Mother Earth and her children and how it has changed lives, affected ministry and fostered kinship responses to the marginalized–human and others alike.

Regarding such ecological sharing (contemporary ecology *fioretti*), there is a particular detail in Francis's *Canticle* that bears closer consideration. While it is significant that Francis calls the creatures brother and sister, even more compelling is his use of Sister *Mother* Earth. In addition, Francis makes clear that he knows this Sister Mother as one who both *sustains and governs:*

Laudato si, mi Signore,	*Praised be You, my Lord*
per sora nostra	*through our Sister*
matre Terra,	*Mother Earth,*
la quale ne sostenta e governa,	*who sustains and governs us,*
e produce diversi fructi	*and who produces varied fruits*
con coloriti fiori ed erba.	*with colored flowers and herbs.*

This then is the *detail*, the specific difference our Sister Mother ought to make in our lives: that we are *consciously sustained and governed by her.* When this insight is put in the context of our ecologically degraded world, it becomes a unique ecofeminist position. Earth governance and earth sustainability provide a fresh way to consider our participation in the larger earth community–not only individually, but also as members of intentional communities. That these words are in the *Canticle* affords them much more than obvious ecological significance. It suggests a particularly Franciscan theological grounding and a particularly Franciscan way of conceptualizing how we *matter.* When our Sister Mother Earth is indeed allowed to sustain *and* govern us, we participate in creating the very conditions whereby more of God's splendor and likeness can be revealed. In the *Rule for Hermitages,* Francis exhorts the brothers to take turns at being both physical and spiritual "mothers" to each other. Perhaps his Canticle image of Sister Mother Earth can also be a reminder that Earth both physically and spiritually "mothers" us. As in the hermitage rule, may it serve to remind us to return the favor.

Applying our Household Skills

Ecofeminist voices variously draw upon insights from goddess cultures, earth-based spiritualities and ecological, bioregional strategies. From the above reflection, it is apparent that there can also be a valid *Franciscan* ecofeminist starting point. If nothing else, our lived experience in the household of our congregations these past fifty years or so has taught us the value of attending to a communal ecology. What might well be ours to do now is the translation of those practices into the broadest possible context–the trans-species Earth community. For the most part, this has never been asked of our religious communities before. We are invited to stretch into this new trans-species incarnation at the same time as we are grappling with painful new community initiations–such as same-species issues of gender impasse and hierarchical marginalizing. Moreover, within the ecology of our communities themselves, our individual members have never been so diverse, so personally empowered and so "seasoned" or so frail.

As we hold together our own contemporary households well, the skills we embody are the very skills that humans need if the species is to be governed and sustained by our Sister Mother Earth. Our community household practices, while resonant with the proto-typical skills of Francis and Clare, are nonetheless necessary innovations in response to the different needs of the time in which we live. Thus, new connections and interpretations are not only appropriate, but also welcome—particularly as they impact theories of individual growth, personal development and spiritual maturation. We welcome these new answers not only for our own members, but for all humans, as we recognize our mutual intrinsic and individual ecological worth. Heretofore unheard-of modes of collaboration, revolution and transformation are therefore invited, not just for the one, but also for the many; not just for my community, but also for the Earth community. Because we have already dared unheard-of modes of collaboration, revolution and transformation for renewed religious life and have thrived, we can dare the same for a renewed Earth household. *Be praised, O God, for Sisters Courage and Experimentation! Of you, Most High, they bear a likeness.*

Conclusion: New Household Loyalties

As we hinted earlier, the household dimension of Clare's spirituality can be useful in presenting a Franciscan ecofeminist position. Clare, like all noble women of her time, was schooled by her mother, Ortulana, and given a formation in the household arts, not the least of which were skills we might associate with community treasurer and refectorian. For Francis, his own mother, Pica, embodied these skills. And at the risk of glib anthropomorphism, I suggest that the image of Pica, and later perhaps of Clare and Jacoba, inspired the "Sister Mother" title given to Earth in Francis's *Canticle.* Francis's life must have afforded him a very tangible experience of a literal and earthly "Sister Mothering."

Clare, too, experienced a very tangible "Sister-Mothering/Mother-Sistering," not only as reluctant abbess to her sisters, but also as daughter of Ortulana Offreduccio, one of her sister Poor Ladies. I am sure anyone who has lived in a family and/or in an intentional community can appreciate the complexity and thickness of such a relationship. Imagine the competing loyalties, the layers of expectation and obligations, the multi-dimensional discernment required for appropriate wholesome action. And this is only in the context of human-human relations. Imagine now Sister Mother Earth as community treasurer and refectorian!

I began this meditation with a kind of ecological map, sharing my own specific household details, my *oikos-logos*–"truth of the home." For me, like for most of my American Franciscan peers, Sister Death hovers near and lends her presence to our lives, not only as she accompanies home our sisters in community, but also as she embraces our land and institutions. Inescapably, we are being nudged to contextualize the dream for the future of our brothers and sisters, not as individual communities or as Franciscans or even as a species. It is nothing less than the dream of our Sister Mother Earth. And amid the confusing tumult of the competing loyalties of my own life–as human, as woman, as American, as Church–it is useful to remember that what is necessary is the vital treasuring of our Sister Mother Earth, who teaches us that we are living and dying in a divine revelatory participation.

So as to support this treasuring and choosing of life as an ecofeminist Franciscan, I affirm the possibility of an earth-appropriate self-transcendence. The numinosity of such a "transcendence" lies in a difference-celebrating, transcending awareness of our mutual household participation. My happy annunciation is that the incarnation of such a household has already begun. Even a cursory survey of the congregations in the Franciscan Federation surfaces many new Earth-caring modes of ministry. Within the larger Franciscan family and beyond, it has taken only a few years to transform peace and justice offices into centers of concern for justice, peace *and* the integrity of creation. When new motherhouse construction is considered, ecological costs are tended, and trees and green space given discerning consideration. Institutions, once presumed permanent, are being transformed for the sake of new life and the future of the household's children, all of them.

I am reminded again of the image of Clare on that Palm Sunday almost eight hundred years ago. There is emerging for me a new significance to the palm branch she receives. Of course, the palm branch continues to signify that she is being invited, like the Christ welcomed into Jerusalem, to participate in the paschal mystery of a new household. Anyone who has ever entered community life knows well the "Perfect Joy," the dying and rising, that such a commitment implies. She is, however, in the receiving of the palm branch, also being recognized for her call by the Church. Thus, it becomes my prayer that all might one day be so recognized. She is in the company of the women of her household. Thus, it becomes my prayer that all may know such mothering/sistering. And finally, my reflection brings me to consider the household Clare is joining. I am sure she had, at that moment, no clue to the extent to which God would give her sisters. As I take the branch my own sister offers me this Palm Sunday, I have no clue, either, as to the household details of the mothering/sistering God will continue to bestow.

Never before has the Franciscan, let alone the human, household been dreamt to be so large and so complex, both in experience and in imagination. Clearly, the implementation of such revised household sensibilities will require of us again heretofore unheard-of loyalties. The sheer magnitude of human biosphere presence demands that we attend to the ongoing "annunciation" of our species' participation in the planetary community that affords us our life. In the course of my Jungian studies, I took great comfort from the intuition Jung inscribed upon his garden gate: "Bidden or not, God is present." The Franciscan *Canticle* tradition likewise assures me that, bidden or not, my brothers and sisters of all colors and species bear the stamp of divine likeness. Human evolution has yet to incarnate satisfactorily such beauty. Our Sister Mother Earth is still awaiting our loyalty. But the good news is this– that the dream of such a possibility has been dreamt, and its beauty, bidden or not, serves to enchant and awe us and bids us do what is ours to do.

Laudato sie, mi Signore, cun tutte le tue creature!

Endnotes

[1]Theodore Roszak, *The Voice of the Earth* (New York: Simon & Schuster, 1992), 233.
[2]There is a veritable chorus of voices presently informing feminist sensibilities. The now classic distinctions of Rosemary Tong, *Feminist Thought: a Comprehensive Introduction* (Boulder, CO: Westview Press, 1989) presents seven of these: existentialist, ecofeminist, liberal, Marxist, psychoanalytic, post-modern and socialist. In addition, there are biblical and post-biblical feminists with their differences as to the oppressive nature of the essential biblical message, as well as the distinctions between feminist theologians per se and thealogians or goddess feminists. Moreover, many feminists, informed by a global political awareness, acknowledge that the "standpoint" consciousness advocated by Mary Potter-Engel and Susan Brooks Thistlethwaite, *Constructing Christian Theologies from the Underside* (San Francisco: Harper and Row, 1990) is the preferred perspective from which to offer a feminist critique.

[3]Charlene Spretnak, "Ecofeminism: Our Roots and Flowering" in *Reweaving the World: the Emergence of Ecofeminism,* ed. Irene Diamond and Gloria Feman Orenstein (San Francisco: Sierra Club Books, 1990), 3-14.

[4]Mary Stewart Van Leeuwen, *Gender and Grace: Love, Work, and Parenting in a Changing World* (Downers Grove, IL: InterVarsity Press, 1990), 130.

[5]Karen J. Warren, "The Power and the Promise of Ecological Feminism" in *Readings in Ecology and Feminist Theology,* ed. Mary Heather MacKinnon and Moni McIntyre (Kansas City, MO: Sheed & Ward, 1995), 172-195.

[6]Judith Plaskow and Carol Christ, eds., *Weaving the Visions: New Patterns in Feminist Spirituality* (San Francisco: Harper & Row, 1989), 1.

[7]Carol Adams, ed., *Ecofeminism and the Sacred* (New York: Continuum, 1993), xi.

[8]Betty Roszak, as quoted in Theodore Roszak, *The Voice of the Earth,* 238.

[9]Ynestra King, "Toward an Ecological Feminism and a Feminist Ecology" in T. Rothschild, ed., *Machina ex dea* (New York: Bergamon Press, 1983), 118-29

[10]Sherry Ortner, "Is Female to Male as Nature is to Culture" in *Women Culture and Society,* ed. M. Rosaldo and L. Lamphere (Stanford, CA: Stanford University Press, 1974), 67-87.

[11]Cf. Mary Daly, *Gyn/ecology* (Boston: Beacon Press, 1978). Daly suggests a revolution of a preferential option for all things womanly. Masculine definitions and devaluations are transcended by her choice to refuse to be limited by them. She ignores them and is not interested in dialogue with the oppressive "other."

[12]Cf. Ingrid J. Peterson, O.S.F., *Clare of Assisi: A Biographical Study* (Quincy, IL: Franciscan Press, 1993).

[13]Arne Naess, a Norwegian philosopher, first coined this term in order to critique the environmental "stewardship" or "conservation" position. Such a position presumes humans have the "right" to do with the biosphere as they wish with only secondary regard for the effect their activities have upon the integrity of other species' lives. The difference between "shallow" and "deep" ecology is exemplified, for example, by the former being willing to set quotas regarding the killing of endangered species while the latter would extend "the rights of man" to all species in a great biosphere-wide egalitarian application. (I have chosen to leave the noun masculine as that is exactly what ecofeminists critique in the deep ecology movement) See Naess's paper, "Shallow and Deep Ecology Movement," *Inquiry* 16 (1973): 95-100.

[14]Bill Devall and George Sessions, *Deep Ecology: Living as if Nature Mattered* (Salt Lake City: Peregrine Smith Books, 1985), 67.

[15]Cf. Naess.

CHAPTER THREE

A CALL TO MUTUALITY
A RESPONSE TO GABRIELE ÜHLEIN, O.S.F.

Dawn M. Nothwehr, O.S.F.

Gabriele Ühlein introduces her "Practical Franciscan Ecofeminist Meditation" by recalling a Passion Sunday celebration. In so doing, she evokes an image and a narrative that confronts us with the paradox of power. There is irony and a bittersweet cast to the celebration because what awaits this momentary "king" is nothing to celebrate. Indeed it is the Roman death penalty, execution on a cross, awaiting Jesus in Jerusalem. But, praise God, this is not the end of the story! In this post-Easter season, we know the empowerment of the resurrection that proclaims that *"power-over,"* oppression and death, do not have the final word. What lives on is a Eucharistic community that engages in a new kind of *"power with,"*[1] born forth from the dangerous memory of One who was *powerful*, because he chose to become *powerless*. This is the power of minority; the power of Francis and Clare; the power that can be ours if we follow in the footprints of Jesus! As feminist ethicist Beverly Wildung Harrison so profoundly states:

> Jesus was radical <u>not</u> in his lust for sacrifice, *but in his power of mutuality*. Jesus' death on the cross, his sacrifice, was no abstract exercise in moral virtue. His death was the price he paid for refusing to abandon the *radical activity* of love–of expressing solidarity and reciprocity with the excluded ones of his community. Sacrifice, I submit, is not a central moral good of the Christian life. Radical acts of love–expressing solidarity and bringing <u>mutual relationships</u> to life–are the central virtues of the Christian moral life.[2]

As I considered Ühlein's meditation from my perspective as a white, U.S., Franciscan, woman, ecofeminist ethicist, I was struck how, at every turn, concerns with power and its dynamics seemed to be at the heart of the question. I will first offer a brief background from my work in feminist ethics concerning power and the notion of mutuality as a formal norm for Christian social and ecological ethics.[3] Not only is this norm deeply rooted in Franciscan theology and spirituality, but also it has probative value for illuminating today's communal, social and ecological issues. Secondly, I will address the four tensions Ühlein sees incarnate in the American Franciscan Federation and respective communities. All of these tensions have roots in various competing cosmologies and theologies.[4]

Even a cursory review of literature in any academic field reveals a radical shift in cosmology, worldview and method. In our own age, all of the sciences reveal a cosmic reality that is an extremely complex network of energies that become consolidated and are then called matter, or are made manifest as pure energy, forming energy fields and morphic fields. We now know that everything and everyone is interrelated. Indeed all of reality must now be understood in terms of its ontological relatedness.[5] God is the All Nourishing Abyss, the Source of All Being. God is in the world and the world is in God. God is a God of Mutual Relation. The images that best describe this cosmic reality are a dance, an arena, or a play. In this view, each component is partly defined in relationship with all other parts of the whole, and the whole cannot flourish in the absence of any one part, yet the whole is greater than the sum of its parts.

If our ontological reality *is* that all is related to everything else, then this impacts what we understand as "the good," who we ought to be and what we ought to do; that is, this reality impacts our ethics. In part, it is this renewed understanding that prompted feminist theologians and ethicists to reconsider the ethics of power. This renewed apprehension of the ethics of power reclaims mutuality as a formal norm for Christian social and ecological ethics.[6]

Traditionally Christian ethics centered on two fundamental principles, love and justice. However, from an ecofeminist viewpoint, the classical theology that undergirded these norms was inadequate because it was patriarchal, never considering women and women's experience to be the normative standard of measure. Thus, it was possible, for example, to call something "just" or "loving" while thoroughly disregarding the perspective of women, the poor, the non-human, or those most affected by an idea or action. However, it is not only *that* one practices love and justice, but also *how* one practices these virtues that makes the difference in the thriving of women specifically and of the cosmos generally. Any such exchange of power needs to be based on the common recognition of the full agency of the other, the concomitant valuing of the other and a common regard marked by trust, respect and affection. In other words, the practice of love and justice requires mutuality. The notion of mutuality must be considered normative and as formative of the foundational moral experience of reverence for human persons and their environment.

Mutuality Defined: What is Mutuality?

From the work of Rosemary Radford Ruether, Elizabeth A. Johnson, Carter Heyward and Beverly Wildung Harrison, it is evident that mutuality is a formal norm for Christian social and ecological ethics and a corrective and a complement to the traditional construal of the norms of love and justice.[7] The reclamation of mutuality by these women is deeply grounded in biblical tradition and in the work of their intellectual ancestors–including Hugh of St. Victor and John Duns Scotus.

Mutuality is a formal norm that can be conceptualized in a manner similar to our understanding of justice, and it is similarly complex. Analogous to those theories of justice which ascribe to it a tripartite nature–contractual, distributive and social–we find four forms of mutuality, namely: cosmic, gender, generative and social.

The basic definition of mutuality adduced from the four feminists is this:

> Mutuality is a sharing of "power-with" by and among all parties in a relationship in a way that recognizes the wholeness and particular experience of each participant toward the end of the optimum flourishing of all.[8]

The first form of mutuality is **Cosmic Mutuality,** defined as

> the sharing of "power-with" by and among the Creator, human beings, all earth elements and the entire cosmos in a way that recognizes their interdependence and reverences all.[9]

Evidence for cosmic mutuality is advanced from the natural sciences including astrophysics, ecology and quantum physics and thereby demonstrates a foundational kinship of everything in the entire cosmos. Also, ecofeminist theory holds that the natural environment asserts itself as a living aspect of "our bodies, ourselves"–it "answers back" when humans defile nature.[10] Humans violate the ecosystem to their own detriment. Cosmic mutuality is grounded in the fact that the most effective social analysis takes into account how any form of power impacts the most disadvantaged, not forgetting all elements of the ecosystem, in the interest of attaining the well-being of all. Traditional Christian cosmology is retrievable to the extent that the relatedness of the created order and the social order is stressed in light of the biblical witnesses. The deep relatedness between God and creation, known as panentheism, has been recognized for centuries as orthodox. The fact that God *is* Creator, Vivifier, or Redeemer only in relation to creation shows, in a certain analogous sense, need on God's part for relationship to the cosmos. Acknowledging the kinship of all creation requires us to consider each non-human as our neighbor, as well. All of this points to *cosmic mutuality.*

Gender Mutuality, a second form of mutuality, is defined as

> the sharing of "power-with" by and among women and men in a way that recognizes the full participation of each in the *imago Dei,* embodied in daily life and through egalitarian relationships.[11]

Gender mutuality is grounded in the fact that women and men are each the bearers of the full *imago Dei* (Gen. 1:27) and they both are capable of full mature moral agency. For the baptized, life in Christ means they are part of a discipleship of equals (Gal. 3:28) that foreshadows the eschatological "New Heavens and New Earth." Jesus' *"kenosis* of patriarchy" is significant because it precludes sexism in any form and because he is the norm for the Christian life. Feminist writers advance biogenic and sociocultural evidence supporting gender equality to challenge classical dualisms and physicalist interpretations of natural law. Evidence from the social sciences also shows social, political, or economic structures can be organized to purposefully empower or disempower women. Finally, all erotic, sensual, embodied knowledge (including sexuality) is a means of God's revelation of Self to us through one another. All of this points to *gender mutuality,* which exists between men and women and is embodied in daily life.

The third form of mutuality is **Generative Mutuality.** The definition of this form is

> the sharing of "power-with" by and among the Divine, human persons and all creation in the on-going co-creation and redemption of the world.[12]

Insofar as each human person bears God's image and likeness within her/his own flesh, each enjoys mutuality with God as co-creator and co-redeemer. The paradigm of the Incarnation itself, Christ Jesus as both human and divine, part of the material world, also lends support to that notion. Indeed, insofar as each creature images God, each participates in the co-creation and redemption of the world. In fact, non-human creation, especially animals such as our pets or farm animals, have a great capacity to teach us the meaning of cogenerativity. Human friendship with God (Aquinas's notion) and the *koinonia* of the baptized are conduits of the co-creative and co-redemptive processes. Images of God-as-Mother suggest understandings of human beings, created in the *imago Dei* as intimately "of my flesh" and "of my spirit." As human children are related to their birth-mother and are empowered and assisted by her to participate in those experiences she judges vital to their well-being, so too, God empowers and assists us toward engagement with Her and one another in activities that further human flourishing in the context of the whole creation. Humans continue to participate in completing the redemption of the world begun by Jesus when they struggle in daily life to establish "right relations." All of this signals that *generative mutuality* exists among the Divine, human persons and all creation.

The fourth and final form of mutuality is **Social Mutuality**. I define this notion as

> the sharing of "power-with" by and among members of society in a way that recognizes the fundamental dignity of each and the obligation to attain and maintain for each what is necessary to sustain that dignity.[13]

As stated earlier, "Jesus was radical not in his lust for sacrifice, *but in his power of mutuality*....Radical acts of love–expressing solidarity and bringing mutual relationships to life–are the central virtues of the Christian moral life."[14] To live as Jesus lived, with a commitment to mutuality, enables us to bear God into the world. That fidelity to mutuality frequently requires making sacrifices for the cause of radical love, creating and sustaining relationships, or righting wrong relationships, and is exemplified by Archbishop Oscar Romero, Dr. Martin Luther King, Jr., Dorothy Day, Rosa Parks and countless others who have suffered for the sake of mutuality but remain nameless. Beverly Wildung Harrison continues:

[I]t is risky to live as *if the commonwealth* of the living God were present—that is, to live by radical mutuality and reciprocity.... Those in power believe such love to be "unrealistic" because those touched by the power of such love tend to develop a reluctance to accept anything less than mutuality and self-respect, anything less than human dignity, anything less than authentic relatedness.[15]

Carter Heyward further qualifies this obligation:

Where there is no effort toward mutuality there is no love. This means that Christians can't love people we don't respect. We cannot love those whom we don't invite to be with us as sisters and brothers. We may pity them; we may treat them charitably; but we cannot love them. . . .Only together, in mutual relation, is there any common personal power, any love, any actual God . . . .The difference between liberal charity and radical love is that, while the former is condescending, the latter is mutual.[16]

The Holy Spirit animates and empowers people enabling them to choose to share in a common *power with* those less powerful or oppressed. The role of the poor must also be stressed. Given the constitutive sociality of the human person, the less powerful are obliged to assert their claim to "power-with" in order to maintain their human dignity. This evidence suggests that *social mutuality* is needed between the powerful and the powerless of our world.

Thus, we have completed a summary definition of mutuality in its four forms. But what does all of this have to do with the four tensions Ühlein named? First of all, I agree that we can find an important link to the norm of mutuality in the life and work of our sister, Lady Clare. As Elizabeth A. Dreyer illustrates, Clare and the Poor Ladies exhibit a sense of self that is secured in a true understanding of the virtue of humility.[17] Confident in the deep and abiding love of God for herself and all others, Clare shows us that such self-understanding "frees one to respect and raise up the 'other'–whether the other be a person or a tree or a paper wasp–as also made and loved by God."[18]

Rooted in the love of God, the relationships of Clare with the Poor Ladies and the "trees, flowers, and bushes" were marked by true affection and friendship, that is, they were distinctively mutual. Though Clare was an "Abbess," she never used the title for herself and rarely exercised the full power over the sisters that the office provided. One might say that Clare exercised her power *with* her sisters, rather than *over* them. In fact, she made provisions in her *Rule* for the Poor Ladies to participate fully in the governance of the community.[19]

While, like Francis, Clare knew a profound respect for human dignity that requires equal regard for all people, she did not neglect the particularities of relating to each of the Poor Ladies according to the requirements of her distinct personality or bodily needs. Quite remarkably, Clare continued to nurture the relationship with the Friars Minor, rather than discount those with whom relations became strained. Clare, rooted in the love of God, continued to reciprocate Francis's pledge to her and the Poor Ladies to give them love, care and solicitude, by extending *her* loving care and solicitude *to* the Friars.

Thus, we glimpse the importance of Clare's lived mutuality as significant for ecotheology. In our world, where the predominant paradigm of relationship is dominance and oppression of the less powerful by the more powerful, both human and non-human, Clare shows a way of engaged, mutual and respectful living. Beginning with the self confidence of one beloved of a God who even cares for the birds of the air and the lilies of the field and a respectful courtly bow to all of creation, Clare shows us a life marked by true deference, love and equal regard, the fruits of which are sensitivity, unity and harmony. It is this kind of living that marks the paradigm to which our civilization must shift if, indeed, our planet is to survive.[20] By being mutually attuned to the "other"–human, non-human or divine–we can achieve the security of life and relationship that is often the goal of those who wield wealth and power over, but which often eludes them.

Mutuality: What a Difference It Makes!

Mutuality makes a great deal of difference in ethics and the outcome of moral discernment. Living in mutuality is an animated process and not a static situation. Set within a dynamic worldview, an emerging feminist ethic of mutuality has implications, first of all, for our *appreciation of truth and truth claims.*

Parties in mutual relationships are oriented to the needs of the other and maintain intentionality directed to the well-being of the other.[21] Mutuality thus requires a *praxis view of truth,* in which the truth is conditioned by the intentions of the relationship.[22] What is true is related to the action-oriented intention of the speaker.[23]

Mutuality is a relationship in which each party has a distinctive particularity and history. Sustaining the relationship requires a *perspectival view of truth,* in which all standpoints determined by culture, gender, history, economics or politics are taken into account. For mutual relations it is necessary to recognize that language is limited in the meaning it can bear. As Wittgenstein has argued, human language can bear only one or two perspectives at once.[24] What is true needs to be understood in a context.

From Gadamer and Ricoeur, there is evidence that knowledge of any text is also an interpretation of the text. In sustaining a mutual relation, this *interpretive view of the truth* needs to be acknowledged lest there be false absolutizing of unintended information or action.[25]

Another kind of truth is *dialogic truth.* As one acts, speaks and interprets with another, there are moments when the "I" and the "Thou" combine to form the "We." It is in those moments that mutuality reaches its apex. If we are not open and ready for these kinds of truth and for the moment of true mutuality that happens in the "between" of dialogue, we live in a false reality, assuming to be the full truth what are indeed only elements of truth.[26]

To understand truth in this way is to gain insight into the **first tension** Ühlein considers, namely: "the painful sensitivity to long-standing, patriarchy-sustaining thinking and methodology." Mutuality *requires* both *broad inclusiveness* and *concrete particularity.* Rather than presuming that the androcentric method, perspective and interpretation can bear the weight of the entire and absolute truth, normative mutuality requires a cosmos-centric perspective that enjoins all parties to bring the myriad aspects of truth together in dialogue to achieve a more complete truth.[27]

Mutuality *shifts ethics' understanding of the moral subject by focusing on the sociality of the human person.* No action can be evaluated as if the person acted in isolation. Moral actions are considered in light of culture, history and the social context of the situation. We are always in a situation of response to others.[28] Our actions make sense only in relationship to others. The structure of a relationship is key to its moral value.

Mutuality also *expands the idea of the moral subject* from one bearing an abstract status (a human nature) to one who develops, experiences and transforms value and who is, in turn, developed and transformed by valuing. The moral capacity of the self, the motivation for sacrifice and justice, is understood in terms of mutuality in relationships.

Mutuality, further, *focuses on reciprocity in moral agency.* In situations of mutuality, the moral subject constantly exchanges valuing and being valued. We are enabled "to grasp our dependence on each other and our social institutions and relations for our moral self-regard and moral power."[29]

Ühlein names "the more recent 'renewal' evolution toward the centrality of personal experience" as a **second tension** in Franciscan life. While she rightly speaks positively of the renewed recognition of the individual, there is a caution to be raised here. The beauty of the vision of Francis was that he recognized the significance of *both* the particularity *and* the relationship of all creatures with God and all others. But, it can be *only one small step* from engaging in a self-initiated ministry to becoming an entrepreneurial proprietary who forgets the good of the whole and one's interdependence with all others. It is necessary that we place ourselves in the position of being influenced by our sisters and brothers; indeed, we need to love one another into an even deeper love of God and all others. As our communities diminish in size and youth, our decisions to continue the dance of mutuality will need to be more intentional and to hold the good of the whole as part of our individual, personal identity.

Mutuality *modifies what is understood as the "good."* Normative mutuality *moves the starting point for ethical reflection to a radically inclusive place,* where literally everyone and everything is included. The moral horizon is the vision of the "New Heavens/New Earth." The present history and the future shape the two-fold context for the vision. "Goods" based on atomistic individualism and patterns of competition, adversarial relations, exploitation, authoritarianism, or paternalism are ruled out because they diminish or deny the fundamental mutual relation that exists between God and humans and that needs to exist between humans, and with all of creation.

Human good needs to fit in with all other "goods" in the cosmos with an eye toward the maximum flourishing of all–not just human thriving. This means mutuality requires an integration of independent and responsible acts as well as interdependent and relational activities. It means that, in achieving the "good," what must be overcome is whatever isolates, completely separates, arouses disinterest and supports atomistic individualism. There is one good that permeates both private and public spheres–mutuality empowers by including everything and everyone in the social/political/economic equation.[30]

Every human is born in need of relationships. When needs and rights are not met and honored, injustice accompanied by self-doubt, mistrust, or resentment occurs. The practice of justice in society also, therefore, needs to include mutual practices of reconciliation.[31] When mutuality is not recognized by both parties and an impasse in relation results, an ethics of care does not abandon the effort. Rather, it moves to confront the deeper blockages and tries again and again. An ethic of mutuality may then knowingly choose to love sacrificially in order to act-the-other-into-life, moving toward greater mutuality.

Surely, the **third tension** Ühlein names as the "newly urgent emphasis on nature and the body" quickly exposes the question concerning what "good" is. Perhaps the epitome of the Body/Spirit dualism shines forth as we face our aging communities and our own inabilities to do the things we used to do. For example: What *"good"* do we experience when a sister or brother is stricken with Alzheimer's disease? Can we see beyond her or his *instrumental* value to the *intrinsic* value of the one God created and now accompanies on the journey of "the long good-bye"? Do we move to adjust our steps in the dance of mutuality to the pace set by the one who no longer remembers? Are we easily able to move from verbal communication to tender looks, gentle touches, or even caring for bodily functions? Can we love for the sake of love and let ourselves be carried into the very heart of Love–the God who loves unconditionally–in mutual relation with every creature for its own sake? It is my belief that when we can find intrinsic value in such a person and allow ourselves to grow in relationship, we will have learned the lesson of embodiment and the meaning of mutuality.

These very lessons in mutual relationship will assist us in setting priorities concerning Ühlein's **fourth tension**: "the ever present difficult choices between the transformation of tradition and the revolution that new paths will require of us." In response to the three resolutions to this dilemma offered by Ynestra King, it seems we Franciscans are called to the way of transformation. Indeed, that is what a life of mutuality requires, that we remain engaged with the "Other" so as to be changed by the relationship. All of us, in every relationship with both human and nonhuman, need to find the equilibrium in the dance of mutuality, taking up and letting go of power that brings about the flourishing of all.

This is the "foolishness" that is beyond human wisdom, but it is the way of the Incarnate One. In the ebb and flow of the power of mutuality, we too find resurrected life. After all, "Jesus was radical not in his lust for sacrifice, *but in his power of mutuality.*"[32] If we are to follow in the footprints of Jesus, we must live mutually. Indeed, mutuality does make a difference in our perception of truth, the moral subject and the moral good. Together these understandings affect our ecological vision of who we ought to be and what we ought to do in relationship with self, God, others and the cosmos.

Endnotes

[1] The term, "power-with" appears early in feminist literature. See Mary Parker Follett, *Creative Experience* (New York: Longman, Green & Company, 1924) and her *Dynamic Administration* (New York: Harper and Brothers, 1942). See Carter Heyward, *Touching Our Strength: The Erotic Love of God* (San Francisco: Harper and Row, 1989), at 191: "Power is the ability to move, effect, make a difference; the energy to create or destroy, call forth or put down. Outside of a particular context, power bears neither positive nor negative connotations. Power can be used for good or for ill. Using power-with others is good. Using power-over others is evil."

[2] Beverly Wildung Harrison, "The Power of Anger in the Works of Love," *Union Seminary Quarterly Review* 36 (1981 Supplement): 52. Italics is Harrison's emphasis, and underlining indicates my emphasis.

[3] See Dawn M. Nothwehr, O.S.F., *Mutuality: A Formal Norm for Christian Social Ethics* (San Francisco: Catholic Scholars Press, 1998). A formal norm is a virtue, an absolute value that indicates what we ought to do and who we ought to be.

[4] Ancient Western cosmology understood the world as a pyramidal structure in which there is a hierarchy of beings, ranging from the most simple and least valuable–stones, plants, animals, human females–to the most complex and perfect–human males, angels, God. Power here is construed as nearly exclusively a "power-over" proposition–human males understood as the most powerful. In Classical Western cosmology, the universe is ruled by a series of deterministic laws that show the marvelous harmony of creation. The world runs like clockwork, God having put everything in its place to function in a specific way. We need only discover those laws and live according to them. Interestingly, the power remains with an elite hierarchy that knows and values these linear and mathematical postulates and devalues or discounts anything else.

[5] See Nothwehr, 1, n.1 See also chapter 2 which illustrates that the grounding of an ethics of mutuality can be found at the heart of John Duns Scotus's Franciscan theology and ethics.

[6] In making this claim, I realize I must deal with the classical "Is/Ought" problem of the naturalistic fallacy. As David Hume showed, one cannot draw a moral "ought" conclusion from a strictly factual or "Is" premise. However, the problem is readily resolved by making explicit any implicit or hidden moral premise and enabling a valid deduction. The main question then concerns the veracity of the premise. See my *Mutuality: a Formal Norm*, especially 1, n.1: "Advances across numerous fields in recent decades can be viewed as recognizing the facticity of mutuality, or even its ontological status." Indeed, it is important to recognize that facts are not value-free nor morally neutral. Significant for our purposes is Jean Porter's claim: "So far from there being a gap between fact and value, there can be no real understanding of the facts that is not simultaneously a knowledge of values."–see Jean Porter, *The Recovery of Virtue: The Relevance of Aquinas for Christian Ethics* (Louisville: Westminster John Knox, 1990), 43-4. Knowledge of what a being really is, is the same as knowledge of what is good for that thing. In this sense, morality is reality.

[7] Here the treatment and use of formal norms is situated within the context of post-Vatican II revisionist Roman Catholic moral theology. The rigorous debate over the absolute nature, the specificity and material content of moral norms has yielded a great deal

of consensus on the possibility of absolute status at the level which is here called "formal." See *Readings in Moral Theology*, No. 1, *Moral Norms and Catholic Tradition*, ed. Charles E. Curran and Richard A. McCormick (New York: Paulist Press, 1979). See also Vincent MacNamara, *Faith and Ethics: Recent Roman Catholicism* (Washington, DC: Georgetown University Press, 1985). In addition, see *Readings in Moral Theology*, No. 2, *The Distinctiveness of Christian Ethics*, ed. Charles E. Curran and Richard A. McCormick (New York: Paulist Press, 1980).

[8]See Nothwehr, 233.

[9]See Nothwehr, 233.

[10]Rosemary Radford Ruether, *Gaia and God: An Ecofeminist Theology of Earth Healing* (San Francisco: Harper, 1992), 2-3: "Ecofeminism brings together . . . ecology and feminism, in their full, or deep forms and explores how male domination of women and domination of nature are interconnected, both in cultural ideology and in social structures." Ruether cites Judith Plant, *Healing the Wounds: The Promise of Ecofeminism* (Philadelphia: New Society Publications, 1989) and Irene Diamond and Gloria F. Orenstein, *Renewing the World: The Emergence of Ecofeminism* (San Francisco: Sierra Club Books, 1990). See Beverly Wildung Harrison, "Politics of Energy Policy," in *Energy Ethics*, ed. Dieter T. Hessel (New York: Friendship Press, 1979), 56.

[11]See Nothwehr, 233.

[12]See Nothwehr, 233.

[13]See Nothwehr, 233.

[14]Harrison, "Power of Anger," 52. Emphasis is Harrison's.

[15]Harrison, "Power of Anger," 53. Emphasis is Harrison's.

[16]Carter Heyward, *Our Passion For Justice: Images of Power Sexuality and Liberation* (Cleveland: The Pilgrim Press, 1984), 167.

[17]Elizabeth A. Dreyer, "'[God] Whose Beauty the Sun and Moon Admire': Clare and Ecology," in Dawn M. Nothwehr, ed., *Franciscan Theology of the Environment: An Introductory Reader* (Quincy, IL: Franciscan Press, 2002), 129-141.

[18]Dreyer, 133.

[19]Clare of Assisi, "The Form of Life of St. Clare of Assisi," 2: 15-18, 21-23; 3: 1-4; 7: 3-5, in *Clare of Assisi: Early Documents*, trans. and ed., Regis J. Armstrong, O.F.M Cap., revised edition (St. Bonaventure, NY: The Franciscan Institute, 1993), 62 note a; 66, 67, 73.

[20]Leonardo Boff, *Cry of the Earth, Cry of the Poor*, trans. Phillip Berryman (Maryknoll: Orbis Books, 1997), 31-34.

[21]See Leonard Swidler, "Mutuality the Matrix For Mature Living: Some Philosophical and Christian Theological Reflections," *Religion and Intellectual Life* 3 (1985): 105-119.

[22]Swidler, 108.

[23]Swidler, 108. Swidler cites the epistemological theories of Max Scheler and Karl Mannheim.

[24]As cited in Swidler, 109.

[25]Swidler, 110.

[26]Swidler, 111.

[27]The danger of relativism can be cared for by identifying presuppositions, acknowledging biases, purposefully seeking out other voices and opinions and probing them for the ways they challenge one, and holding modesty as the highest virtue. In the Christian community, the focal coherence of scripture, traditions, and the *sensus fidelium* can provide additional safeguards.

[28]H. R. Niebuhr, *Responsible Self: an Essay in Christian Moral Philosophy*, paperback edition (New York: Harper and Row Publishers, 1978), 70-71.

[29]Ruth L. Smith, "Morality and Perceptions of Society: The Limits of Self-Interest," *Journal for the Scientific Study of Religion* 26 (1987): 289.

[30]Smith, 288-91. It could be argued that the formal norm, mutuality, actually

disempowers one because human finitude does not allow any person to *always* deal with *everything* and *everyone*. While humans are indeed limited, the purposeful creation and maintenance of community, solidarity, friendship, ecological and spiritual relationships can assist one in staying focused on the goal of an evermore perfect praxis of mutuality. In the Jewish and Christian contexts, it is understood that God's grace undergirds all efforts toward perfect mutuality. (Recall for example Buber's notion of the Eternal Thou and Duns Scotus's notion of *acceptatio*.) In the case of non-believers, human reason concerning a course toward basic survival and a high quality of life can provide the impetus for striving toward a more perfect praxis of mutuality. Like the formal norms of love and justice, mutuality provides a standard and source of motivation, inspiration, vision and instruction. Not to consider mutuality, however, is to neglect a whole realm of moral responsibility and possibility.

[31]Margaret Catroneo, "A Contextual Catholic Ethics," Ph.D. diss. (Philadelphia, PA: Temple University, 1983) at 248: "The dialogue context requires that each partner be able to state his or her needs and expectations to the other in terms of the present. It is a process of mutual accountability. Reestablishing a dialogue on this basis in an injured relationship is a form of giving. By asking for something, a person says he or she continues to care enough about the relationship to risk rejection. It is the extending of trust in order to open up the possibility of rebalancing the 'ledger' of exploitative or unjust relation through the reciprocal giving of the other. Giving through asking is a claim on the other for reciprocal consideration of one's own needs and expectations. Because the claim is in the form of asking, it is an acknowledgment of the other's capacity for trustworthy giving."

[32]Beverly Wildung Harrison, "The Power of Anger," 52. Emphasis is Harrison's.

CHAPTER FOUR

TAKING NATURE SERIOUSLY: NATURE MYSTICISM, ENVIRONMENTAL ADVOCACY AND THE FRANCISCAN TRADITION

Keith Douglass Warner, O.F.M.

Locus enim est principium generationis rerum.
(For place is the origin of things.)
Roger Bacon, *Opus Maior*

What is our responsibility toward creation? This is an excellent and timely question for us to address as Franciscans. But before we do so in earnest, I would like us to take a step back and ask: what is our responsibility as participants in the Franciscan Intellectual Tradition (FIT) project toward the broader mission of the Franciscan Movement? The strategic plan for the FIT[1] has provided an inspiring vision of how we might make ourselves available to the Franciscan Family and the Church as public intellectuals. The plan suggests ways we might prepare men and women in the classroom, but also undertake popular education projects to enhance our fidelity to the Franciscan charism. We have a long history as religious educators providing service in a variety of settings, but this vision we are working to implement has the capacity to enhance our collective fidelity as a Franciscan Movement. This is very exciting for me.

And for many others as well! Quite a few friars have expressed to me enthusiasm for the work we are doing, and not just friars who have specialized academic training. This project has transformative potential because it has the ability to enhance the lived vocational experience of the lives of our brothers and sisters. We are constituting ourselves more clearly than ever as a community of scholars with a shared Franciscan identity. We are describing with greater specificity and relevance the Franciscan world vision. We are articulating this vision to the broader membership of the Franciscan Family. This is all very, very good cooperative action. One additional crucial linkage is with our

53

Franciscan socio-political project, and I would like to make my professional contribution in this context.

The work of Franciscans International (FI), the Justice, Peace, and Integrity of Creation offices of the Friars Minor (JPIC) and similar outreach by other institutions are the chief institutional expressions of our Franciscan socio-political project. This is some of the most important work we do as a Franciscan Movement. In addition to the tasks already identified in the strategic plan for the FIT project, I think we would do well to put our intellectual resources at the service of the hundreds and thousands of Franciscan men and women engaged in this work around the globe.[2] This tripartite project of promoting peace, justice and the integrity of creation expresses the values our Father Francis brought to his encounter with the world. Francis's conversion was profoundly religious, but from this core experience, he imagined more peaceful, respectful and reverential relations between God, humans and the natural world.

Our Franciscan spiritual tradition intersects with the most compelling socio-ethical global needs in the three arenas. Since the eighth centenary of Francis's birth, the Franciscan Family has made substantial progress in its justice and peace work, both in terms of conscienticizing our communities and engaging with broader efforts to promote humanistic values.[3] Our work for social justice is founded, in part, on Francis's meeting the leper, for this encounter stimulated his own conversion and his efforts to promote compassion and radical inclusion in his preaching and ministry. Our work for peace is firmly rooted in Francis's peacemaking both within and between the Italian *communes* and between Christians and Muslims.

But what about our work on behalf of creation? This is definitely the weakest of the three components. Justice and peace are strongly related to each other, but concern for creation seems to straddle several dimensions of Franciscan life: our socio-political advocacy, our contemplative practices and our tenuous tradition of studying the natural sciences. From what I can tell, there have been a few writings on the unraveling of our biosphere and a very few individual members of our movement who have undertaken environmental advocacy initiatives; but compared to the other two components of our project, care for creation doesn't rank.[4] This deficiency is especially surprising given that our Pope named Francis the patron saint of ecology. I have reflected at length on our shortcomings in this area since becoming a friar, and I welcome this opportunity to continue this reflection.

The reasons for the Franciscan Family's paucity of interest in creation are complex, subtle, interconnected and largely assumed. Our global environmental crises spring from problematic assumptions about and systematic disregard for nature. Confused ideas about nature afflict our Franciscan brothers and sisters just as they do most people in the advanced capitalist societies. We have skills and resources that can help others perceive and understand relationships presently not well recognized. As a family, we are seriously hampered by a restricted understanding of nature and a lack of imagination in the spiritual and scientific realms.

Anthropogenic disturbance of global climatic systems and collapsing global biological diversity pose fundamental challenges to the very future of human society, along with global patterns of violence and economic inequity. These planetary ecological meta-trends threaten the life support system of our planet–soil, water, air, nutrients, energy flows are all being disrupted.[5] This erosion of our planetary life support systems may be irreversible. Before full "scientific proof" can be amassed, it will be too late to prevent a series of humanitarian and ecological catastrophes. The risks they pose are most definitely not arrayed equitably; they imperil the life of the poor disproportionately. In a world where forty percent of the people live on two dollars per day and social development is stalling or backsliding, environmental disruption looms ominously.

This is a very appropriate time for us to reflect on the nature-oriented theological resources in our tradition, on the problematic qualities of nature-society dualisms that we have unconsciously acquired and on what kinds of scientific communities we might be able to engage as allies. It is time to formulate action plans for carrying out a Franciscan socio-political project that can enhance the protection of our natural world. So, as a crude response to the question posed in the conference title, I suggest our responsibility is to:

1. pray with nature
2. learn from nature
3. act on behalf of nature.

But those activities pre-suppose that we take nature seriously as an agent of religious conversion and as an object of our interest and compassion.[6] I hope that my contribution here will help us strengthen and configure our intellectual resources to develop and articulate a way for us to take nature seriously, especially in its material, dynamic and relational qualities. In this paper I will reflect on nature's agency in the Franciscan vocation, report from critical social science disciplines on revolutions in thinking about nature-society relations that could be of great assistance to our work, identify some public interest ecological scientists whose work we could articulate with our Franciscan Intellectual Tradition and suggest some action items to further our socio-political project to take nature and its needs seriously.

How Nature Prompted My Franciscan Vocation and Why That is Awkward

Not being raised Catholic, I first learned about Francis of Assisi when I was eighteen years old through Franco Zeffirelli's *Brother Sun, Sister Moon*. In the late 1970s, many social values were being renegotiated, at least in California, and this film provoked me to much reflection. Francis's approach to discipleship fascinated me, and I saw the movie three times in one weekend. Six months later, I left the University of California—Davis—and joined an ecumenical lay community of about forty men and women who had moved to rural Oregon to establish a discipleship-training program. Manual labor in orchards and forests was an integral part of this program. Every fall we sent out teams to harvest apples and pears in the Pacific Northwest. Winter and spring would find us in the mountains reforesting clear cuts. Apple picking and tree planting are wonderfully sensate experiences of nature. We lived very simply and worked very hard, and this strengthened our community and our spiritual lives. We lived in common, shared all our income and were very close to nature. I do not mean to romanticize these experiences, however, because the work was very demanding physically, and we lived on the brink of material want.

In September and October our crews lived in migrant worker housing adjacent to the orchards. We would walk out the door and into the agricultural work environment. We felt good about working in a natural setting that was providing food for people. Fruit harvesting, though difficult, is a joyfully simple and social task. Tree planting is quite a bit more demanding physically. We would typically work in rain and slush on hillsides that were steeper than I had thought possible and carry thirty-plus pounds of seedlings strapped to our hips through all manner of brush, logs, brambles and rockslides. This is one of the most demanding forms of manual labor, equal to oil derrick work. Yet it seemed like the right thing to do. We were putting baby trees back in the forest—what could be more virtuous?

A little bit of ecological learning can be subversive, however. After several years in the woods, I began to investigate the impacts of the kinds of clear cutting that our reforestation crew was following. Large transnational corporations were systematically removing biologically diverse forest ecosystems and replacing them with monoculture tree farms. And we were participants in that system. Information about the environmental impacts of industrial forestry was beginning to make its way into the media. Whatever virtues we were practicing by our tree planting, this was part of a bigger system that was seriously harming the health of these forests.

I began to realize what a tremendous gift it was to have spent that much time intimately engaged with the forest. I loved the diversity, relief, beauty and vitality of the Pacific Northwest forests. When an injury forced me out of the woods and into urban employment, I came to appreciate just how deeply my five seasons in the wilderness had impacted me. I had spent days upon days under the open sky repeatedly plunging my hands deep into mother Earth. I had spent weeks at a time scrambling around the cliff-like Oregon hillsides in the ever-present winter rain. In springtime we would ascend with the snowline to the high Cascades and on to the Rockies where we could plant into the summer. I was witness to the full cycle of seasons in the Pacific West, and this changed me as a person. At a corporeal level, I began to realize prayer was not a recitation of words or intention but a "living in relationship with." Spending most workdays in wilderness silence re-oriented my prayer away from a recitation of my desires and toward a stance of affection. I was one creature among a whole watershed of others, many of which we humans were not treating well. I learned about relationships of mutual support and assistance both within my community and between humans and nature, and convictions about the ethics of care took root in my life. The landscapes of such beauty worked their way into my soul. God's love found expression in the beauty of those landscapes. Prayer in nature became an integral part of my life. Nature was no longer the abstraction I had studied in school, but rather material and dynamic, and I felt related to it in ways that I could not fully explain.

I relate this story for two purposes. First, nature has been an agent of my conversion. I would not have seriously considered a Franciscan religious vocation had I not had such a season of initiation into contemplation. I probably would have been a Francis-inspired advocate for justice and environmental protection, but that is only one dimension of

Franciscan religious life. Second, my relationship with creation was made concrete by this period of manual work in nature. For me, environmental problems are not abstract. I still have a relationship with Western forests and orchards. Environmental threats to their viability are very real to me because those places have been important to my life and spiritual development. When I read our Franciscan sources about people-nature interactions, I bring the lenses of my own experiences.

Three years after my tree-planting career ended, the lay community to which I had belonged was coming to a close. For two of those years, I had been engaged in the corporal works of mercy with Franciscan men and women and decided the Franciscan Friars provided the best place for me to continue to pursue my social and spiritual dreams. I was impressed by the work of John Quigley (St. John the Baptist Province) in the area of Justice, Peace and the Integrity of Creation (JPIC). Upon returning to California, I was interested in environmental education and advocacy but didn't really know what might be possible. I worked with a remarkable vocation director, a specialist in horticulture, who had just finished a Master's thesis providing a liberation theology critique of Amazon forest destruction.[7] Naturally, he encouraged my interests, but was not in a position to promise anything. I completed a bachelor's degree in Geography and Environmental Studies prior to joining the Order, and during my candidacy year I interned at an environmental organization.

In my initial years of formation, I received various reactions to my desire to integrate spiritual and environmental concerns. Some were dismissive, some uninterested. Many persons responded with curious looks.[8] Some acknowledged the value of such an integration, and a few actively supported and encouraged me. One wise senior friar who had lived and served in the Pacific Northwest for virtually all his religious life suggested that I might really be able to help the Franciscans with this kind of work. I was dubious, but heartened by his words. Seven years into religious life my provincial encouraged me to pursue advanced studies, and four years ago I began a doctoral program in Environmental Studies with an emphasis on agroecology.

Looking back, based on what I know now about the orientation, formation and propagation of religious life in the United States over the past century, I should not have been so taken aback by the scant support I received for this "novel" professional interest. Maybe I shouldn't have been scandalized. But from my reading of Franciscan books, I knew that Francis was a nature lover. It disturbed and discouraged me that I found so little "loving of nature" in the fraternity I was joining. This was all the more striking given the social context of the Pacific West. I have shared my interest in this integration of nature and spirit with countless lay Catholic peers, and the responses have been: "That's great!" "A natural fit for Franciscans and environmentalism," "Are there more like you?" (which might be translated: "Are you a normal Franciscan?")

Regardless of how one feels about Lynn White's influential essay, *The Historic Roots of our Environmental Crisis,*[9] we as a Franciscan Family need to acknowledge a significant popular expectation that Franciscans devote some attention and resources to address environmental crises. In the American West this is an expectation held by Catholic, Protestant and secular people alike. Perhaps this is a regional phenomenon. Perhaps I am a strange creature from Ecotopia.[10] If this were some "West Coast cultural thing," we could ignore it. But it isn't and we can't. These issues are not going away; they are getting worse and increasingly intractable. Environmental values may be regionally variable, but we ignore this expectation to our peril. We are witnessing a broad scale cultural shift. Are we going to participate in it?

A few years ago Franklin Fong, O.F.M., and I did a series of presentations around the Pacific states about over-consumption and Francis's love of nature. I was surprised and very pleased at the enthusiasm people brought to these workshops and the depth of their understanding of environmental problems. We spent some time talking about Francis's nature mysticism and participants responded enthusiastically. People responded particularly passionately to the opportunity to integrate their love of nature with their Christian faith. I sensed that we offered them a rare space in which to do that integrative work. This feedback motivated me to re-dedicate myself to this kind of work and explains part of the reason I returned to graduate studies. I realized I was participating in one expression of American cultural evolution, but to contribute substantively I was going to have to do more work of personal integration. However, I don't want my professional work to be just about me, but rather about us as a Franciscan movement.

There is a split between popular expectations about Franciscans valuing nature and my lived experience in Franciscan religious life. What is our responsibility to listen to these expectations? How might ignoring them harm the integrity of our Franciscan mission in the world? Why do other groups seem to be more excited about Francis as the patron saint of ecology than the Franciscans?

On Francis as a Nature Mystic and
Why that Term Might Not Matter

Before I began academic studies in theology, I had always assumed that Francis was a nature mystic. He loved nature and encountered God in nature, and that was good enough for me. I soon discovered that mysticism is a specific type of spirituality, about which there is a good bit of academic controversy. Nature mysticism in particular is very difficult to define satisfactorily. Scholars differ in their fundamental assumptions about individuals and the kind of interior psychological and spiritual experience they undergo, their perception of nature and their understanding of the relationship between nature and God. Thus, it may not be possible to assert that Francis was a nature mystic; but I think this question is important for us as Franciscan academics to investigate, keeping these divergent assumptions in mind.

The first problem we confront is that Francis never claimed for himself any kind of mystical experience in nature. The *Canticle of the Creatures* is the only notable text attributed to Francis himself that speaks about nature, and even though one can easily imagine it as the fruit of many days in prayer in nature, he makes no claims about any special experiences. Another problem is sorting out the differences between animals and elements in Francis's experience. The *Canticle* gives more emphasis to elements, but his hagiographers wrote in more detail about animal encounters.

When we turn to the secondary sources and the animal stories,[11] we face a number of problems in their interpretation. *St. Francis of Assisi and Nature* by Roger Sorrell is still the best work on this subject. He offers a provocative re-interpretation of Francis preaching to the birds. He asserts that the import of this encounter is the effect it had on the saint, basing this on Thomas of Celano's theological reflection at the end of the story.

> After the birds had listened so reverently to the word of God, he began to accuse himself of negligence because he had not preached to them before. From that day on, he carefully exhorted all birds, all animals, all reptiles, and also insensible creatures, to love the Creator, because daily, invoking the name of the Savior, he observed their obedience in his own experience (1C 58).

Sorrell argues that this experience served to integrate Francis's views of nature with his understanding of himself as preacher and that it resulted in a "new outlook" on creation. The most important implication of the story is not that he preached to birds but the impact that birds had on him.[12] This is a form of "reverse mission," in which the preacher is in fact the person most evangelized. Does Sorrell's argument stand up to scrutiny? What other evidence do we have that inter-species encounters impacted Francis?

William Short offers us guidelines for studying hagiographic method in saints' animal stories. This work investigates the long tradition of authors employing animal stories to communicate the holiness of saints. By the eighth century, a series of conventions had coalesced around the interactions of saints and animals, drawn from various Scriptural and spiritual traditions. Animals recognize and respond to the presence of Christ in the saints; they revere the saints; paradise is restored in the presence of the saints; the obedience of the saint to God evokes the obedience of animals to the saint; peace between animals and humans is renewed; in short, cosmic order is restored.[13] These were the standard motifs deployed by hagiographers to communicate their message: the saint is powerful and holy.

The majority of the elements of animal stories in Thomas of Celano's writings are in fact drawn from this tradition. That Thomas used stories of interactions with animals to make his point is much less important to my interests than examining any novel dimensions. How does Thomas describe the impact of these interactions on Francis?

The following table lists only the animal stories in Thomas's work that describe an impact on Francis. Several themes not common to hagiographic conventions emerge. Francis relates to animals as brothers and sisters (1C 59 and 61). Francis learns or practices humility as a result of interacting with animals (1C 58 and 2C 171). Francis reaches out to "feed" animals with food or the word of God (1C 58, 59 and 80). Francis experiences love and compassion as a result of interactions (1C 60 and 80; 2C 47, 167 and 111). Notably absent from these stories are demonstrations of power or commands to creatures to act obediently (other than asking the birds to listen to his sermon).

Encounters with animals from Thomas of Celano's *Life of St. Francis* and *The Remembrance of the Desire of a Soul* that describe an impact on Francis.	
Animal	**Encounter**
Birds	1C 58: Francis preaches to birds, but realizes his responsibility to preach to all creatures. 1C 59: Francis's preaching cannot be heard so he silences the swallows and addresses them as "sisters." 2C 47: Francis rejoices over feeding robins and their brood and curses their one greedy offspring. 2C 167: Francis holds a bird, lifts up his eyes, remains in prayer and returns to himself. 2C 168: Francis is grateful to a falcon for not waking him for early vigils when he is ill. 2C 170: Francis tests a pheasant's devotion to him.
Rabbit	1C 60: Francis is moved to tenderness by a trapped rabbit, asking the rabbit why it was caught.
Fish	1C 61: Francis generally throws back a caught fish, and when one fish is given to him to hold, he blesses it and calls it "brother."
Worms	1C 80: Francis has a "warm love" for them and picks them up from the road.
Bees	1C 80: Francis extols them and feeds them wine.
Cricket	2C 171: Francis sends an obedient cricket away so as to avoid any boasting on his part.
Lamb and sow	2C 111: Francis is moved to compassion by the death of an innocent lamb and curses the merciless sow who killed it.

That Francis's heart was moved by animals is perhaps the most interesting theme because it is common in Thomas's corpus and novel to the hagiographic literature. The following passage is of particular import because it relates an especially powerful encounter.

A fisherman offered him a little water-bird so he might rejoice in the Lord over it. The blessed Father received it gladly, and with open hands, gently invited it to fly away freely. But the bird did not want to leave: instead it settled down in his hands as in a nest, and the saint, his eyes lifted up, remained in prayer. Returning to himself, as if after a long stay in another place, he sweetly told the little bird to return to its original freedom (2C 167).

This story is unlike others related by Thomas for the kind and degree of impact the animal has on Francis. It describes Francis going to "another place" in prayer while having direct, sensate contact with an animal. Thomas offers no conclusion about the theological import of this story. The way this story is related by Thomas suggests it was not fully comprehensible to him. It may be one of the "dangerous memories" of the early companions that did not sit comfortably with him. The unusual nature of this story argues for its authenticity.

These stories related how animal encounters moved Francis in his heart, gave him an experience of warm love, provoked him to compassion and led him to take some action to protect their well- being. Taken as a whole, these appear to support Sorrell's assertion that Francis's relationship with nature was novel. His relating to nature in a spiritual way was not new, but the impact that these interactions had on him does appear to be something new. Adopting a conservative scholarly approach to nature mysticism precludes an affirmation of Francis being a nature mystic because we do not have evidence from Francis himself about such an experience. If one uses popular criteria for being a nature mystic, such as an experience of God in nature, he certainly qualifies. If the term "nature mystic" troubles some scholars, we can set it aside for academic reasons. The accounts of Francis's spiritual experiences in nature—the animal stories, stories of his encounters with the elements of sun, fire and water and stories about the time he spent in wilderness hermitages—do communicate the importance of this dimension of his religious life. Nature was alive in Francis's life. It had agency.

Francis's experiences in nature were not the only elements of his life that were novel to Christian spirituality. Ewert Cousins asserts that Francis's spiritual experiences were novel in their devotional, Christocentric character. He describes this approach as "mysticism of the historic event," in which one "recalls a significant event in the past, enters into its drama and draws from it spiritual energy, eventually moving beyond the event towards union with God."[14] Is it too much to claim that elements of nature played a role analogous to historical events in Francis's prayer life? And should we consider this innovative? A brief review of the religious imagination of the twelfth century may offer some helpful context.

Medieval European people perceived and made sense of reality in ways that are quite foreign to contemporary Americans.[15] Compared to the medieval world, "objective reality" as we understand it today is much more restricted due to the Enlightenment, rationalism and scientific and psychological revolutions. From a popular perspective, theirs was an enchanted world, one they implicitly understood to be much more complex than could be apprehended through sense perception. They were more comfortable correlating the ordinary with the spiritual and the superstitious. They understood visions, dreams, encounters with spirits, religious experiences at shrines, talismans and unusual events as reinforcing their beliefs in a spiritual world that they could not fully perceive. Among learned clerics, Augustinian Platonism provided the dominant theological understanding of the material world with its distinction between the perfect, infinite, ultimate reality and the world that can be seen and observed with the senses.

As M.-D. Chenu has demonstrated so admirably, the twelfth century was a time of increasing intellectual sophistication.[16] Scholasticism was forming, and at the same time, scholars were confronting nature in a new way. A poetic or exclusively symbolic understanding of nature was giving way to proto-scientific investigations and writings. Scholarly interests transcended what the Scriptures and the ancients said about nature and started to observe the biology of living organisms. Nature began to be described as a system, as a whole, with an ordered unity. Chenu links this "re-discovery of nature" with the widespread use of the term *universitas*. Interest in the natural world moved beyond bestiaries to the systematic observation of nature investigating the causes of things. Belief in miraculous causes gave way to scholarly preference for natural explanations. Medieval society was waking up to nature's material reality and its utility for the emerging market economy; theological dimensions of nature were a part of this interest.

I believe Francis's relationship with nature can best be understood in this context–nature as an "enchanted" world full of living creatures, interacting in a family-like system.[17] In this world, nature definitely had agency and played an active role in Francis's process of conversion. His relationships with nature and with lepers were equally material and

dynamic, and his process of religious conversion was profoundly relational—he was moved to compassion (*pietas*) by contact with both. To
me, someone without formal philosophical training, the Neoplatonic
view of nature seems very far from Francis's approach. Neoplatonism
tends to view nature in an abstract way, focusing on universal essence
rather than on concrete matter. The divergence between Francis's view
and the Neoplatonic view heightens my unease with our contemporary discussions about cosmologies because, in my understanding of
Francis's imagination, he did not think abstractly. Nature was not a
philosophical/theological concern for him. Nature consisted of a living
community that he experienced through his senses, and he relished these
experiences, encountering God in nature just as he did in lepers. It is no
surprise that the notion of *haecceitas* springs from a spiritual tradition
initiated by a founder who relished encounter and relationship with
"the other," human or otherwise. Nature is experienced by the whole
person—it is not an idea.

Yet I repeatedly hear Neoplatonic assumptions about nature when
Franciscans and others speak about Francis. Organisms and elements
in nature are not considered specific entities unto themselves. They are
not *haec*, but rather are symbols indicating a "more real" reality in some
other abstract place. In this view, nature is a storehouse of theological
symbols. These assumptions imply we somehow need to look through
or beyond nature to encounter an abstract God. These assumptions about
nature set the stage for a devolution to the sentimentalism and romanticism that now dominate the views of nature held by some members of
the Franciscan family and many others in the faith community. These
assumptions, when fused to the Cartesian worldview, reinforce a utilitarian evaluation of nature and, when fueled by capitalism, underlie a
relationship with nature that facilitates the unraveling of the biosphere.
Neoplatonic assumptions blind us to perceiving nature as material,
dynamic and relational.

Revolutionary Thinking about Nature-Society Relations

Within and across multiple social science disciplines and the humanities, scholars are undertaking a vigorous re-examination of the relationship between society and nature.[18] This has been stimulated by increasing concern over the depth and breadth of environmental crises and
has focused on this question: what epistemological assumptions have
fostered and are now accelerating the ecologically destructive behavior
of human society? These scholars argue that social theory has for too

long ignored the materiality and agency of nature; and in the few examples of acknowledging nature's agency, it has been conceived of within a binary framework, which again reproduces a flat, passive understanding of nature. In this section I hope to bring in a "report from the fields" of other disciplines, especially environmental history, geography, science and technology, in the hopes that it can stimulate some new thinking about our Franciscan tradition and "the matter of nature."[19]

Historians, analyzing earlier work by their colleagues, now recognize that these had assumed nature to be dead, passive or simply a backdrop for "real" history, which consisted only of human activities. Prior to 1970, history had frequently been written as if human beings were not really a part of a living planet, as if the human experience was without natural constraints, or as if climate, disease, soil quality, biogeographic variation and the invasion of species were without impact on human society.[20] Environmental historians discovered nature to be material, relational and dynamic. This recognition gave rise to the field of environmental history, which brings an ecological perspective to the study of human societies through time.[21]

It was a study of the most dramatic collapse of an ecosystem in U.S. history that marks the emergence of this approach—Donald Worster's *Dust Bowl: The Southern Plains in the 1930s*.[22] Two other early works examined New England—William Cronon's *Changes in the Land* and Carolyn Merchant's *Ecological Revolutions*.[23] Both of these works are significant for they broaden the historian's perspective beyond an exclusive interest in political and intellectual history to include nature's role in human affairs. Nature is no longer conceptualized as empty wilderness but rather a peopled landscape; nature is no longer primordial but rather present and shaping the development of human society.[24]

This research thrust has required historians to employ additional methodological tools and become versed in the ecological sciences. As a result they have become more reflexive and critical about nature-society relations.

> Ecological thinking constructs nature an active partner. The "nature" that science claims to represent is active, unstable, and constantly changing. As parts of the whole, humans have the power to alter the networks in which they are embedded. Nature as active partner acquiesces to human interventions through resilience and adaptation or "resists" human actions through mutation or evolution. Nonhuman nature is an actor;

human and nonhuman interactions constitute the drama. Viewed as a social construction, nature, as it was conceptualized in each social epoch (Indian, colonial and capitalist), is not some ultimate truth that is gradually discovered through the scientific processes of observation, experiment and mathematics. Rather, it is a relative subtle shift in the structure of human representations of "reality." Ecological revolutions, I argue, are processes through which different societies change their relationship with nature.[25]

In *The Death of Nature*, Merchant investigated the process by which European society shifted its views of nature from the "enchanted world" to nature as mechanical, utilitarian and dead. Environmental problems are not new, she argues, but their scale, degree and risk have grown tremendously. Merchant casts light on the problematic assumptions of the mechanical revolution and the Enlightenment and leads her fellow historians in critical self-reflection on their field, its purpose and its prospects.[26]

Environmental historians are now fleshing out the neglected side of the nature-society dualism. This ecological approach to history explicitly assumes that societies arise within nature, that nature offers multiple trajectories for the development of societies and that nature expresses agency by intervening in human affairs in varied ways. It explicitly rejects assumptions that nature is a passive object to be acted upon. As Margaret FitzSimmons and David Goodman suggest, nature should be understood as both internal *and* autonomous, as causal *and* contextual, and always consequential.[27] Similar critical self-analysis has taken place throughout the social sciences, but especially in environmental sociology, feminist anthropology and geography.[28]

Among these scholars, a deep discontent with dualism has arisen. Geographers such as Jacque Emel and Jennifer Wolch argue that dualistic thinking hobbles our ability to perceive agency outside the human realm.[29] I follow Val Plumwood's definition of dualism: "The construction of a devalued and sharply demarcated sphere of otherness."[30] Feminist scholarship in particular has shed light on the way dualistic thinking relies on exclusions, denials of interdependency, arguments for instrumentalism, objectification and stereotyping. Dualism is useful at an elementary level of learning; comparisons can be a helpful pedagogical tool. But dualistic thinking about nature-society relations produces the simplistic and flawed thinking that fetters our relationship with nature.

Dualism creates false compartmentalization, inherently privileges one party at the expense of another, re-enforces the human being as a unitary subject and chains us to the juggernaut of instrumentalism.[31] Dualistic thinking underlies the anthropocentric thinking that has emerged since the Enlightenment. Dualism relegates nature to a passive landscape. It is pernicious precisely because it is largely unconscious.[32]

The divide between society and nature, between people and animals, has been artificially constructed, but is now showing signs of fraying. In contemporary society, dualistic thinking predisposes people to mental categories of "jobs versus the environment," as though an economy were possible without a healthy ecosystem. Agriculture and businesses are starting to model their practices on ecological process.[33] Even the ontological separation of humans and animals is showing signs of strain. "Critiques of post-Enlightenment science, greater understanding of animal thinking and capabilities, and studies of human biology and behavior emphasizing human-animal similarities have all rendered claims about human uniqueness deeply suspect."[34]

Geography has long held an interest in studying the relationships between people and nature. In recent years, critical human geography has pursued investigations into the social, economic and scientific institutions that shape nature/society relations.[35] In this analysis, these institutions largely shape "the rules" about what humans do with nature and, implicitly, our assumptions about nature, especially in the primary sectors of the economy such as agriculture, forestry and fishing. This scholarly community has investigated nature's agency also, exploring specifically the role that science and its disciplines have played in shaping our understanding and assumptions. One early and brilliant example is David Harvey's "Population, Resources and the Ideology of Science." Harvey raises critical questions about the ethical neutrality of science and "the" scientific method advanced by some scientists, especially in the population/resources debates. He argues that when positivism and logical empiricism define one's assumptions about resource shortages, Neo-Malthusianism is the result. He asserts that Western thinking about "overpopulation" is shaped more in assumed political ideologies than "scientific truths."[36]

More recent work in human geography has been influenced by Science and Technology Studies (STS). Early work in this field was based on anthropological studies of scientists in laboratories and the social conditions of the production of scientific knowledge.[37] In contrast with earlier works in the philosophy of science that tended to revere individual scientists, STS focuses on the credibility, authority and social roles of scientists and scientific knowledge.[38] Michel Callon did pioneering work on the relations between marine ecologists, fishermen and scallops that drew attention to the different ways that these actors express agency within a socio-ecological network.[39]

Geographers and other social scientists interested in nature and ecological questions have used STS and Actor-Network Theory (ANT) with considerable success to break down assumptions about nature's passivity and the "ignorance" of farmers, fishermen and peasants who lack "scientific" understanding.[40] Some have used these methodologies to unmask the social and epistemological stances assumed by scientists in their modeling of global climate change. Critics raise important questions about how uncertainties and assumptions about international economic justice tend to become obscured in these debates.[41] Collectively, research efforts like this are re-invigorating human geography, raising critical questions about the role science, scientists and technology play in society and breaking open new ways of imagining nature/society relations.

I conclude this section with some propositions for how we might use these developments in other disciplines to shape a more complete Franciscan theology of nature. Dualistic thinking, like Neoplatonic assumptions, blinds us to how we conceptualize nature as a flat and passive backdrop, as something less than alive. Taking nature seriously should spur us to understand how material, dynamic and relational qualities shape nature's relation to society.

First, all humans are part of nature, and nature includes all humans. Too much emphasis has been placed on making nature the "other," and this has confused our understanding of the inter-relationship between humans and nature. Human society is fully enmeshed in the natural world. Noel Castree recommends the term "socionature" to clarify this relationship.[42] Assumptions that nature is "out there" and not "in here" are inherently flawed.[43]

Second, there is no such thing as "pure" nature, in wilderness or anywhere else. There is no part of the globe that has not been directly or indirectly impacted by human civilization. The few "biological islands" remaining, whether legally designated wilderness or not, are indeed crucial for biodiversity protection, but all landscapes host life in various forms of complexity and degrees of "naturalness." Wilderness areas are rare and important and deserving of full protection, but we should not ignore nature's various forms in all landscapes. American beliefs about the "purity" of wilderness obscure more than they enlighten.[44] Assumptions that nature is "less present" in mixed-use landscapes than in the Brazilian Amazon or in the Arctic National Wildlife Refuge are highly problematic, for they reproduce dualistic thinking yet again.

Third, all humans participate in socio-ecological systems. Life is not possible without ecological relationships. We all depend on the food, air, energy and water that nature provides. Some human lifestyles may obscure this dependency, but it is nevertheless a reality.[45]

Fourth, agriculture is the most extensive hybrid socio-ecological activity on the face of the earth. It is the primary metabolic relationship between human society and nature.[46] Even in the most thoroughly disturbed agricultural systems, nature is present, too.[47] Some refer to this as "second nature," referring to the human-guided ecological succession processes that take place in agroecosystems.[48]

Fifth, human societies have always employed technologies that impact nature and the ecosystems upon which we depend for life.[49] Environmental problems are not new, but their scope and severity are. American society in particular seems to be loath to reconsider the so-called "progress narratives," which insist that the human-technology relationship we currently have is the best, most rational and most enlightened that a society could possibly have—and this is inevitable, too, for other cultures. Our society steadfastly refuses to question the social and ecological costs of our obsession with technology. North Americans in particular seem unable to accept the idea that previous societies enjoyed a good quality of life. Through our assumptions, our culture actively reproduces a false dualism between ours and past societies.

Sixth, science and the scientific method do not exist independent of society, nor the social relations of scientists to that society.[50] For all their genius, generosity and manifold contributions to societal well-being, scientists do not appear any more or less capable of escaping the prejudices of their cultures than any other human beings. This appears to be particularly true when science is employed in the service of capitalism. In this regard, scientists participate in what Bruno Latour calls "techno-science," or the production of scientific knowledge to create and market technology.[51]

Attending to the Children of Rachel

William Short, O.F.M., offers the opinion that nature is too important to be left only to the care of scientists, and I could not agree more.[52] Other commentators suggest that the recent convergence of interests between religion and science is one of the most important trends of the past century. Many books have been written on this subject, generally ending with a plea to continue the dialogue.[53] But if one wants to engage in this conversation, one is immediately confronted with several questions: dialogue with whom? about what? and why? Science is a very big house with many portals. Inside, one finds many different kinds of social actors engaged in many different kinds of activities with wildly divergent ends. Cold calling on the academy can be frustrating.

Most of these science-theology conversations have addressed the important questions of the origin of the universe, theology and evolution, and the ethics of genetic interventions.[54] This is important work, but I would like to suggest a particular community of scientists with a particular set of interests to the broader Franciscan Movement. Because nature played such an important role in Francis's religious life, because of the grave threats to our global environment and because our founder has been named the patron saint of ecology, I recommend that we engage specifically with those whom Margaret FitzSimmons calls public interest ecologists.

Ecology as a discipline has some characteristics that distinguish it from other scientific pursuits. More than any other discipline, it attends to the negative environmental impacts of anthropogenic technological introductions. Ecology generates scientific knowledge that pertains to the common good, because ultimately, environmental crises affect the global commons. Ecologists are among the least likely to generate proprietary knowledge, which is, sadly, now a dominant tendency within U.S. universities.[55] Ecology frequently concerns itself with studies of the troubling history of employing technology and the unintended consequences of disrupting ecosystems. Ecology suggests the value of a precautionary principle that suggests a "look before you leap" criterion.[56]

Those who direct society's attention to the negative environmental consequences of technology are apt to be persecuted like prophets. The controversy surrounding DDT and Rachel Carson's *Silent Spring* illustrates this.[57] And yet courageous men and women continue to research and write about these kinds of problems. I recommend two works that carry on in Carson's tradition. Theo Colborn, Dianne Domanowski and John Peterson Myers investigated the invisible and poorly understood impact of endocrine disruptors, which disrupt the development of reproductive organs and threaten the future of both animal and human life.[58] Joe Thornton researched the continued impact of artificial industrial toxins as they are bioaccumulated in the top predators of ecosystems, behaving similarly to DDT.[59] The work of these authors identifies problems in critical, applied social ethics. They document how transnational corporate interests profit by releasing toxic substances at the expense of other cultures, future human societies and other organisms today. These ecologists have been subject to withering criticism by monied interests that resent the publication of information exposing the negative environmental impacts of industrial products.[60]

The work of such ecologists is only one manifestation of the public interest scholarship being done today. The Ecological Society of America (ESA) is the leading U.S. professional scientific organization of ecologists. Over the past ten years it has sought to marshal its collective intellectual resources to educate key social and political leaders about the impact of human behavior on the environment. In 1991, it issued a report, "The Sustainable Biosphere Initiative," which spelled out a research agenda for this disciplinary community. This outreach effort has three priorities:

1. Global change
2. Biological diversity
3. Sustainable ecological systems, including the interface between ecological processes and human/social systems

The ESA conducts research and education around these programmatic areas at all levels, from the most technical and theoretically sophisticated down to fact sheets accessible to high school students and everything in between. These are all available free on the world wide web.[61] Unlike most scientific disciplines, the ESA has created a structure to communicate with the broader public about public interest issues. The organization has engaged in a variety of other initiatives aimed at strengthening its ability to make professional resources available to the public and to present an agenda of actions society should take to address environmental problems. FitzSimmons studied the ESA's Sustainable Biosphere Initiative and noted that it emerges from a coordinated effort on the part of ESA leadership to imagine how, as an institution, ESA could contribute to addressing socio-ecological problems.[62] This involves connecting their organization's academic resources with potential allies in society at large and in NGOs, identifying research priorities and communicating their collective understandings to several audiences outside their immediate disciplinary community.

Both the Sustainable Biosphere Initiative and the Franciscan Intellectual Tradition project are examples of research planning. I find remarkable the parallels between these two. The "Strategic Plan with Recommendations to the ESC-OFM" should be seen as a breakthrough for the development of our Franciscan academic community. I commend the efforts to strengthen the institutional cooperation of our various study centers, to articulate a Franciscan vision of the world and to promote the valorization of scholarship that is not exclusively theological in its orientation.

I am most grateful for our tradition being recognized as "intellectual" rather than "theological," for, of course, it is not exclusively theology. We have scientists in our family, both past and present, and they have made important contributions; but they are not well known. Two of particular note are Robert Grosseteste (d. 1253) and Roger Bacon (d. 1292). Grosseteste never actually joined the friars because he was appointed Bishop of Lincoln, but he and the early English Franciscans influenced each other extensively.[63] He studied and wrote about poetry, music, architecture, mathematics, astronomy, optics and physics. One of his students, Roger Bacon, an educational reformer and a major medieval proponent of experimental science, joined the Franciscan Friars in 1252. A student of astronomy, alchemy and languages, he supported vigorous educational reforms. He described the process for making gunpowder and envisioned flying machines and motorized vessels. He wrote on the tides and recommended a reform of the calendar.[64] He proposed that Asia could be reached by sailing west and developed a system of coordinates for terrestrial geographic use, which laid the foundation for later map projections.[65] Bacon learned from careful observation of nature, describing its properties and behavior, and he connected this scientific knowledge with theology, education and ethics. He was an interdisciplinary scholar. He might very well be named the patron saint of Franciscan geographers.[66]

Now more than ever we need Franciscans like Roger Bacon. His approach to education and nature can help guide the urgent work that the world—including nature!—needs from us. How can we act on behalf of nature? First, we all need more education—a different kind of education. Human societies are going to have to learn their way out of our crisis. Second, we need to partner with other people who share our values. I believe public interest ecologists would like to partner with us. We actually do have resources that would be of interest to them. As Franciscans, we have a certain kind of moral legacy. This can be used for good. We have skills in helping promote reflexivity that are of interest to scientists; this is a theme that comes up with some consistency in the science/religion dialogue literature, and it could be of service to the public interest ecologist community. Third, we are leaders in communities of people who are favorably disposed toward moral discourse. Public interest ecologists, too, are interested in reaching out to "communities of ethical concern." This could be a kind of mutual education project—Franciscans and public interest ecologists working together—and could bear much fruit for advocacy on behalf of nature.[67]

I have described here three scholarly communities and their engagements with nature and the environment. Many social scientists have "discovered" nature and have made substantial progress including it in their analyses. Some natural scientists understand their contribution to include engaging institutions and individuals concerned about the ecological health of their society. And for us Franciscan academics? In Francis we have a patron who took nature seriously in his religious journey. How will the Franciscan Intellectual Tradition project take nature seriously?

What is Ours to Do?

As Franciscan scholars we can serve our Franciscan Family by putting our intellectual resources at the service of other Franciscans: to give them hope, to speak to their fears and to present a coherent intellectual pathway that strengthens faith and encourages just action for our neighbors.[68] We can best achieve this by recovering the historical elements of our tradition, but also by using skills honed by this history to engage the contemporary social and ecological issues. At this time, I believe we are in greater need of a shared understanding of nature and the threats it faces than of more writings on a theology of creation. Genuine developments in theologies of creation cannot come without a greater shared understanding of nature and the threats it faces.

Recovering our intellectual tradition is a holy undertaking, and to be truly successful we will have to work with a new level of cooperation, both among ourselves and with other scholarly communities. In this final section, I would like to itemize how I hope to express that mission through my professional contribution, and I would invite any and all with similar interests to join in this venture. These activities can only be successful as part of a common project.

With Franciscan academics:

1. We have much more work to do in elaborating the practical implications of our Franciscan view of creation. Ilia Delio, O.S.F., has written a helpful synthesis of its philosophical characteristics,[69] but the Franciscan movement needs a more complete articulation of how our tradition can engage the socio-ecological needs of the world today. We can help the Franciscan movement free itself of the problematic assumptions prevalent in the broader U.S. society: Neoplatonic abstractions, dualism, utilitarian thinking and the romanticism and sentimentalism which cloud our relationship with nature. These all serve as major obstacles to constructive engagement with the forces driving our environmental problems. We Franciscan scholars need a revolution in thinking about nature similar to that undertaken by environmental historians and geographers. This work can result in shared understandings of the problem and in bringing our resources to environmental education and advocacy. It can help connect our theologies of creation with the material, dynamic and relational qualities of nature.

2. How can we better put our academic skills at the service of our brothers and sisters on the forefront of our collective socio-political project on Justice, Peace and the Integrity of Creation? Concern for creation is but one aspect of this tripartite project. Franciscan intellectuals could have a profound impact if they put their skills at the service of Franciscans International and the work of the committee on JPIC. The FIT project could co-sponsor a meeting with FI and/or with the JPIC committee. This would be another stage in our FIT research planning. We could also explore how we could better contribute to the work of the National Religious Partnership for the Environment.[70]

3. We can encourage interdisciplinary scholarship. The credibility of our Franciscan witness in the world is enhanced when our members receive advanced training in the natural or social sciences, especially when we do this in preparation for public intellectual work. In our individual education ministries and our formation work, we could encourage other Franciscans to undertake this work.

4. We can encourage every Franciscan with any intellectual interest to familiarize him or herself with basic ecological principles, beginning with the accessible ESA work identified above.

5. As Franciscans we must contribute to thinking critically about the role of technology in our societies. Some forms of technology enhance human dignity, but many have negative environmental impacts, which harm nature today and future human generations. We should undertake initiatives to study and educate members of our Franciscan movement about using technology more judiciously and about the socio-political choices societies can make regarding the direction of technological research.

With Franciscan study centers and institutions:

6. How can we better promote courses at our educational institutions devoted to concerns for justice, peacemaking and environmental protection? All Franciscan study centers should teach, at a minimum, a class on "Environmental Literacy for Religious Leadership." They could also weave concern for the environment into other courses.

With Franciscan leadership:

7. Provincials and other leaders in the Franciscan movement are in key positions to encourage members to take nature seriously. Leaders could encourage individuals to pursue studies in this area, especially in the sciences. They could designate a "creation animator" in local communities to promote resource stewardship and awareness of environmental issues. They could propose the development of hermitages, which would allow those living in them to intensify consistently their relationship with nature as did our father St. Francis, but also facilitate prayer

in nature for those seeking to pray in more secluded natural settings. The renewal of the contemplative dimension of our vocation is integrally related to taking nature seriously.

8. Franciscan leadership could promote the development of educational and advocacy initiatives about nature, both within provinces and congregations, but also as a form of social outreach. Many corners of society are waiting for Franciscans to make a substantive contribution to advocacy on behalf of the environment, and there are younger men and women attracted to the Franciscan movement who want to contribute to this work. How can we create appropriate, cooperative ministry structures to facilitate this outreach?

9. Franciscan leadership could encourage Franciscan institutions to initiate stewardship initiatives, using resources more judiciously, allowing a greater role for nature and for the enhancement of natural beauty. Environmental audits help identify areas of concern, opportunities for ministry and resource conservation possibilities.

With local Franciscan communities:

10. Taking nature seriously at the local level could have many different expressions. It could be the focus of contemplative days of recollection. It could be the object of study in terms of environmental problems. Actions on behalf of nature could include environmental clean-up days and efforts to landscape. All of these activities allow nature to have agency in our lives and to facilitate our on-going conversion. Spending time in nature has great potential for being re-creative.

11. Given the radical poverty of our founder, we Franciscans would do well to be known for preaching simplicity of life. This theme in our outreach would be true to our tradition and very timely given the social and ecological problems our world faces.

With scientists of good will:

12. We can be of service to public interest ecologists. With even a modicum of study of ecological issues, we could undertake a fruitful inter-institutional dialogue. But first we would need to read and to listen. Several scientific communities are interested

in promoting greater reflexivity among their members, and our religious training could be of help here. Striving for humility and the practice of contemplative prayer would be of interest to them. In addition, we could partner with public interest ecologists to help them reach a broader segment of society and, in so doing, lend additional legitimacy to their efforts to advocate a more sustainable world.

Acknowledgements: Many thanks to Ilia Delio, O.S.F., for organizing this symposium! This essay has been enhanced by conversations with Bill Short, O.F.M., Joe Chinnici, O.F.M., James Lockman, O.F.M., and Margaret FitzSimmons. Mark Schroeder, O.F.M. and Bill Fontenot, S.F.O. provided helpful feedback.

Endnotes

[1]ESC-OFM, *The Franciscan Intellectual Tradition Project* (Pulaski, Wisconsin: 2001).
[2]The strategic plan wisely connected the FIT project with the Franciscan educational needs of the developing world.
[3]Several Franciscans with advanced academic training have made critical and substantive contributions to JPIC work. Examples include: Louie Vitale, O.F.M., and his work promoting nonviolence with the *Pace e Bene* Center; David Couturier, O.F.M. Cap., *Franciscans International and a Cry of the Poor in an Age of Terrorism*, An Address to the North American Capuchin Conference (New York, 2002). Cf. also, Michael Crosby, *Spirituality of the Beatitudes: Matthew's Challenge for First World Christians* (Maryknoll: Orbis Books, 1981); *House of Disciples: Church, Economics, and Justice in Matthew* (Maryknoll: Orbis Books, 1988).
[4]Some works in this area are: Margaret Pirkl, O.S.F., *One Earth, One World, One Heart*; Dawn Nothwehr, O.S.F., *Franciscan Theology of the Environment: An Introductory Reader* (Quincy: Franciscan Press, 2003); Gabriele Ühlein, O.S.F., *Meditations with Hildegard of Bingen* (Santa Fe: Bear & Co., 1984); "Creation: A Franciscan Conversion Conversation," *In Solitude and Dialogue: Contemporary Franciscans Theologize*, ed. Anthony Carrozzo, O.F.M. (St. Bonaventure, NY: The Franciscan Institute, 2000). Should we be surprised that this is an area where Franciscan women are making a greater contribution than men?
[5]Cf. Peter M. Vitousek, Harold A. Mooney, Jane Lubchenco and Jerry M. Melillo, "Human Domination of Earth's Ecosystems," *Science* 277 (1997): 494-499.
[6]The very word "nature" is, however, one of the most complex in the English language. Raymond Williams distinguishes three specific but closely related meanings of the word:

    a. The ontologically essential or necessary quality of something.
    b. The inherent force which directs either the world or human beings or both. In so far as these natural laws, in the sense of (b), determine the quality and nature, in the sense of (a), of something, there is some overlap between nature (a) and (b).
    c. The external, material world itself (e.g., the material world).

Cf. Raymond Williams, *Keywords: A Vocabulary of Culture and Society* (London: Flamingo, 1983), 219. In this essay I am limiting my discussion of nature to meaning (c). I am indebted to David Demeritt for his analysis of this term. Cf. "Being Constructive About Nature," *Social Nature: Theory, Practice, and Politics,* ed. Noel Castree and Bruce Braun (London: Routledge, 2001), 22-40.

[7]Cf. James T. Lockman, "Reflections on the Exploitation of the Amazon in Light of Liberation Theology," *Covenant for a New Creation: Ethics, Religion, and Public Policy,* ed. Carol S. Robb and Carl J. Casebolt (Maryknoll: Orbis Press, 1991), 165-195. Also *The Exploitation of the Amazon in Light of Liberation Theology* (Berkeley: GTU Dissertation, 1988).

[8]A few friars have expressed to me their discomfort with Matthew Fox's approach to Creation Spirituality, which they have perceived to be an excessive critique of mainstream Catholic theology. This discomfort appears to be much more prevalent among Franciscan religious men than women due to the form of their theological training. The work of Matthew Fox and Brian Swimme has been extremely helpful for calling Christian theology to emphasize the creation-centered elements in our tradition; however their approach does not appear to have much traction with many who have undergone graduate theological training for ministry. For a critique of Creation Spirituality and how Franciscans need to emphasize an alternative, incarnational approach, see Keith Warner, O.F.M., "Out of the Birdbath: Following the Patron Saint of Ecology," *The Cord* 48.2 (1998): 74-85.

[9]I am hesitant to refer to the work of Lynn White, "The Historical Roots of Our Ecological Crisis," *Science* 155 (March 10, 1967): 1203-1207. It is filled with errors. He wove facts and prejudices together seamlessly, and his arguments have become hackneyed. The article set off a flurry of theological counter-arguments, which is good; but in our efforts to engage the Franciscan Family with the issues of nature and the environment, we would do better to start elsewhere. Cf. J. Baird Callicott, "Genesis and John Muir," *Covenant for a New Creation: Ethics, Religion and Social Policy,* ed. Carol S. Robb and Carl J. Casebolt (Maryknoll: Orbis Press, 1991), 107-140.

[10]Cf. Ernest Callenbach, *Ecotopia Emerging* (Berkeley: Banyan Tree Books, 1981).

[11]Space considerations require me to limit my analysis of secondary sources to Thomas of Celano's first two works, but other important texts include Bonaventure's *Major Legend,* 8:6-10, and *Mirror of Perfection,* Larger Version, 113 and 118. All references to early Franciscan documents in this paper are from Regis J. Armstrong, O.F.M. Cap., Wayne Hellmann, O.F.M. Conv., and William J. Short, O.F.M., eds., *Francis of Assisi: Early Documents,* Volumes 1-3 (Hyde Park, NY: New City Press, 1999-2001).

[12]Roger D. Sorrell, *St. Francis of Assisi and Nature* (New York: Oxford University Press, 1988), 55-68.

[13]William J. Short, O.F.M., "Hagiographic Method in Reading Franciscan Sources: Stories of Francis and Creatures in Thomas of Celano's *First Life* (58-61)," *Greyfriars Review* 4.3 (1990): 63-89. Also, by the same author, *Saints in the World of Nature: The Animal Story as Spiritual Parable in Medieval Hagiography (900-1200)* (Rome: Pontificia Universitas Gregoriana, Facultas Theologiæ, Institutum Spiritualitatis, 1983).

[14]Ewert Cousins, "Francis of Assisi: Christian Mysticism at the Crossroads," *Mysticism and Religious Traditions,* ed. Steven T. Katz (New York: Oxford, 1983), 166.

[15]Cf. Carolly Erickson, *The Medieval Vision* (New York: Oxford, 1976).

[16]Cf. Marie Dominique Chenu, *Man, Nature, and Society in the Twelfth Century* (Chicago: University of Chicago Press, 1968).

[17]For Francis, nature was "creation," but for ourselves, we cannot escape the influence the sciences have had on our societies and their worldviews. I have intentionally avoided the use of the term "creation" in this essay, in part because I want to focus the attention of the Franciscan movement more on the material qualities of nature and reframe our theological understanding of nature in that light.

80   Keith Douglass Warner, O.F.M.

[18]Cf. Noel Castree and Bruce Braun, *Social Nature: Theory, Practice, and Politics* (London: Routledge, 2001). By the same authors: *Remaking Reality: Nature at the Millenium* (London: Routledge, 1998).

[19]Cf. Margaret FitzSimmons, "The Matter of Nature," *Antipode* 21.2 (1989): 106-120.

[20]Cf. Donald Worster, "Transformations of the Earth: Toward an Agroecological Perspective in History," *The Journal of American History* 76 (1990): 1087-1106. This is one of several important contributions to this issue on environmental history in this special issue. Cf. also Donald Worster, *The Ends of the Earth: Perspectives on Modern Environmental History* (New York: Cambridge University, 1988).

[21]This group of environmental historians also discovered that they needed new methods to engage these questions, and I suggest that in the same way we Franciscans do, too.

[22]Cf. Donald Worster, *Dust Bowl: The Southern Plains in the 1930s* (New York: Oxford University Press, 1979).

[23]Cf. William Cronon, *Changes in the Land: Indians, Colonists, and the Ecology of New England* (New York: Hill and Wang, 1983). Also Carolyn Merchant, *Ecological Revolutions: Nature, Gender, and Science in New England* (Chapel Hill: The University of North Carolina Press, 1989).

[24]Cf. Margaret FitzSimmons and David Goodman, "Incorporating Nature: Environmental Narratives and the Reproduction of Food," *Remaking Reality: Nature at the Millenium*, ed. Bruce Braun and Noel Castree (New York: Routledge, 1998), 194-220.

[25]Merchant, *Ecological Revolutions: Nature, Gender, and Science in New England*, 23.

[26]Cf. Carolyn Merchant, *The Death of Nature: Women, Ecology and the Scientific Revolution* (San Francisco: Harper Collins, 1980).

[27]FitzSimmons and Goodman, "Incorporating Nature: Environmental Narratives and the Reproduction of Food," 197.

[28]For an excellent and accessible introduction, cf. John Barry, *Environment and Social Theory* (New York: Routledge, 1999).

[29]Cf. Jacque Emel and Jennifer Wolch, *Animal Geographies: Place, Politics and Identity in the Nature-Culture Borderlands* (London: Verso, 1998).

[30]Val Plumwood, *Feminism and the Mastery of Nature* (New York: Routledge, 1993), 45.

[31]Emel and Wolch, *Animal Geographies: Place, Politics and Identity in the Nature-Culture Borderlands*, 63.

[32]Val Plumwood, *Environmental Culture: The Ecological Crisis of Reason* (New York: Routledge, 2002) 45.

[33]Cf. Stephen R. Gliessman, *Agroecology: Ecological Processes in Sustainable Agriculture* (Chelsea, MI: Ann Arbor Press, 1998). Also, Paul Hawken, Amory Lovins and L. Hunter Lovins, *Natural Capitalism: Creating the Next Industrial Revolution* (Boston: Little, Brown and Co., 1999).

[34]Emel and Wolch, *Animal Geographies: Place, Politics and Identity in the Nature-Culture Boderlands*, 63.

[35]Cf. Clarence J. Glacken, *Traces on the Rhodian Shore: Nature and Culture in Western Thought from Ancient Times to the End of the Eighteenth Century* (Berkeley: University of California Press, 1967); John Leighley, *Land and Life; a Selection from the Writings of Carl Ortwin Sauer* (Berkeley: University of California Press, 1963). Also, Margaret FitzSimmons, "Geographies: Engaging Ecologies," *Envisioning Human Geographies*, ed. Paul Cloke, Philip Crang and Mark Goodwin (London: Edward Arnold, 2003).

[36]David Harvey, "Population, Resources, and the Ideology of Science," *Economic Geography* 50.3 (1974): 256-77.

[37]Cf. Bruno Latour and Steve Woolgar, *Laboratory Life: The Social Construction of Scientific Facts* (Thousand Oaks: Sage, 1979).

[38]Cf. Bruno Latour, *Science in Action: How to Follow Scientists and Engineers through Society* (Cambridge, MA: Harvard University Press, 1987); Sheila Jasanoff, Gerald E.

Markle, James C. Petersen and Trevor Pinch, eds., *Handbook of Science and Technology Studies* (Thousand Oaks: Sage Publications, 1995).

[39]Cf. Michel Callon and John Law, "On the Construction of Socio-Scientific Networks: Content and Context Revisited," *Knowledge and Society: Studies in the Sociology of Science Past and Present*, ed. Lowell Hargens, Robert Alun Jones and Andrew Pickering, vol. 8 (London: JAI Press, 1989), 57-83; Michel Callon, "Some Elements of a Sociology of Translation: Domestication of the Scallops and the Fishermen of St. Breiuc Bay," *Power, Action and Belief: A New Sociology of Knowledge?*, ed. John Law (London: Routledge & Kegan Paul, 1986), 196-233.

[40]Actor-network theory (ANT) as developed by Latour, Callon and Law, overcomes the analytical dualism of nature versus culture by rejecting a priori agency for humans alone. Cf. Sarah Whatmore, "Hybrid Geographies: Rethinking the "Human" in Human Geography," *Human Geography Today*, ed. Doreen Massey, John Allen and Philip Sarre (Cambridge: Polity Press, 1999), 186-202. They suggest three principles that underpin ANT: (1) following actors through their activities as they move through their network; (2) the natural and the social must be explained together; (3) actors can join together across a number of conceptual divisions such as local/global or social/technical. Cf. Judy Clark and Jonathan Murdoch, "Local Knowledge and the Precarious Extension of Scientific Networks: A Reflection on Three Case Studies," *Sociologia Ruralis* 37.1 (1997): 38-60; Jacquelin Burgess, Judy Clark and Carolyn Harrison, "Knowledges in Action: An Actor Network Analysis of a Wetland Agri-Environment Scheme," *Ecological Economics* 35 (2000). ANT has been very influential in nature/society studies, but it is not without critics. Cf. Noel Castree and Tom MacMillan, "Dissolving Dualisms: Actor-Networks and the Re-Imagination of Nature," *Social Nature: Theory, Practice and Politics*, ed. Noel Castree and Bruce Braun (London: Routledge, 2001), 208-224.

[41]Cf. David Demeritt, "The Construction of Global Warming and the Politics of Science," *Annals of the Association of American Geographers* 91.2 (2001): 307-337; Stephen H. Schneider, "A Constructive Deconstruction of Deconstructionists: A Response to Demeritt," *Annals of the Association of American Geographers* 91.2 (2001): 345-348.

[42]Cf. Castree and Braun, *Social Nature: Theory, Practice, and Politics*.

[43]Cf. FitzSimmons and Goodman, "Incorporating Nature: Environmental Narratives and the Reproduction of Food."

[44]Cf. William Cronon, ed., *Uncommon Ground : Toward Reinventing Nature* (New York: W. W. Norton & Co, 1995).

[45]Cf. Sarah Whatmore, *Hybrid Geographies* (London: Sage, 2002).

[46]Margaret FitzSimmons, "The Social and Environmental Relations of U.S. Agricultural Regions," *Technological Change and the Rural Environment*, ed. P Lowe, T. Watson, and S. Whatmore (London: David Fulton, 1990), 248.

[47]A confrere reported on a conversation he had with an African missionary at an international Franciscan educators' meeting about my interest in environmental studies. The missionary believed that the environment was of concern only to privileged people in rich societies until my confrere explained to him that I was studying the relationship between environmental health and agricultural sustainability. Nature should not be seen as exclusively instrumental, but it definitely can be.

[48]William Cronon, *Nature's Metropolis: Chicago and the Great West* (New York: W. W. Norton & Co., 1991), 52.

[49]Cf. Merchant, *The Death of Nature: Women, Ecology and the Scientific Revolution*.

[50]Cf. Bruno Latour, *We Have Never Been Modern* (New York: Harvester Wheatsheaf, 1993); also, *Pandora's Hope* (Boston: Harvard University Press, 1999).

[51]Cf. Sheldon Rampton and John Stauber, *Trust Us, We're Experts!* (New York: Penguin Putnam, 2001).

[52]William J. Short, O.F.M., personal communication.

[53]Cf. John E. Carroll and Keith Warner, O.F.M., *Ecology and Religion: Scientists Speak* (Quincy, IL: Franciscan Press, 1998).

[54]This literature is vast. For recent works, cf. John Haught, *God after Darwin: A Theology of Evolution* (Boulder: Westview Press, 2000). See also, Ted Peters, *Playing God? Genetic Determinism and Human Freedom* (New York: Routledge, 1997), *Science, Theology and Ethics* (London: Ashgate, 2003), and Ted Peters and Gaymon Bennett, *Bridging Science and Religion* (London: SCM, 2002).

[55]Cf. Eyal Press and Jennifer Washburn, "The Kept University," *The Atlantic Monthly* (March, 2000) http://www.theatlantic.com/issues/2000/03/press.htm (2000).

[56]Cf. Lawrence Busch, "The Homiletics of Risk," *Journal of Agricultural and Environmental Ethics* 15 (2002): 17-29.

[57]Rachel Carson, *Silent Spring* (New York: Houghton Mifflin Co., 1962). Paul Mueller–who invented DDT–received the Nobel prize; Rachel Carson did not.

[58]Cf. Theo Colborn, Dianne Dumanoski and John Peterson Myers, *Our Stolen Future: Are We Threatening Our Fertility, Intelligence, and Survival?: A Scientific Detective Story* (New York: Dutton, 1996).

[59]Cf. Joe Thornton, *Pandora's Poison* (Cambridge: MIT Press, 2000). He did this research while staff scientist for Greenpeace.

[60]Cf. Rampton and Stauber, *Trust Us, We're Experts!*

[61]The main webpage for the "Issues in Ecology" series is: http://www.esa.org/sbi/sbi_issues/. I recommend in particular issue #4, "Biodiversity and Ecosystem Functioning: Maintaining Natural Life Support Processes." The ESA education office also offers shorter fact sheets on these topics, such as global climate change, at http://www.esa.org/education/resources/factsheets.php.

[62]I am indebted to Margaret FitzSimmons for this analysis. Cf. FitzSimmons, "Geographies: Engaging Ecologies."

[63]Cf. James McEvoy, *Robert Grosseteste* (New York: Oxford University Press, 2000).

[64]"Roger Bacon," *Science, Optics and You* (NA), http://micro.magnet.fsu.edu/optics/timeline/people/bacon.html (2003).

[65]Cf. David Woodward, "Roger Bacon's Terrestrial Coordinate System," *Annals of the Association of American Geographers* 80.1 (1990): 109-122.

[66]Roger Bacon's work was embraced by his Franciscan leadership with ambivalence. A contribution of his was condemned by the minister general for "suspect novelties" and he was imprisoned. Those who articulate relationships between the sacred and secular do risk resistance from certain kinds of religious authority.

[67]The Biodiversity Project has excellent resources to assist with this kind of ethical communication. Cf. http://www.biodiversityproject.org/publications.htm, especially: Biodiversity Project, *Ethics for a Small Planet* (Madison: Biodiversity Project, 2002), and Lowry, Suellen and Rabbi Daniel Swartz, *Building Partnerships with the Faith Community: A Resource for Environmental Groups* (Madison: Biodiversity Project, 2001).

[68]Cf. ESC-OFM, *The Franciscan Intellectual Tradition Project.*

[69]Cf. Ilia Delio, O.S.F., "A Franciscan View of Creation," Franciscan Heritage Series Vol. 2 (CFIT) (St. Bonaventure, NY: Franciscan Institute Publications, 2003).

[70]Cf. http://www.nrpe.org/

CHAPTER FIVE

A FRANCISCAN VIEW OF CREATION
A RESPONSE TO KEITH WARNER, O.F.M.

Franklin Fong, O.F.M.

From yesterday's discussions and presentations we have been challenged by philosophical, theological and scientific approaches to breaking open the theme of this symposium–Franciscans and Creation. The approach so far has been from a systematic reflection and study of philosophical principles and theological constructs, ecological theories and socio-political perspectives as to how Franciscan spirituality may give us a different lens to understand, appreciate and simply be in the world around us. Through such a diversity of ways of understanding, we are then called and challenged to become stewards of the gifts of the physical and biological world.

I will take this opportunity to present a different lens to view the world around us. I want to share with you some of my reflections on the past ten years and what it has meant for me as a biologist, a teacher and an academic researcher to become a religious and a Franciscan at the mid-point of my adult life. I share these experiences with the humility of someone on the road to Emmaus. I share them with you in particular as a fellow pilgrim on a faith journey. I share them with you in awe and amazement at how God has touched me in the most unexpected grace-filled moments. As a scientist, I can say that the moment of clarity is identical to those moments when I was able to look at some cluster of data or at some event and perceive, in the coming together of disparate events and facts, some other underlying force or principle which accounts for the results.

Let me explain first why I will be using the image of a lens to piece together my reflections. A lens gives us the ability, on the one hand, to magnify an object of study. By flipping a lens over, we can view a larger area and see an object in the context of its immediate surroundings. A lens is not a prism that takes a single beam of white light and separates it into its component and constituent elements. A lens is not a mirror that reflects back to us our own image. A lens is not a screen that filters out some part of an image. A lens enables us to see the relationships between parts of a larger object, though these relationships may appear distorted.

The most common lens allows us to peer through with one eye at a time. Certainly more expensive versions are available which allow binocular vision. But here we will use a single lens, which means that we can see with only one eye, one perspective, one angle at a time. It also implies that we are able to separate out different perspectives. The lenses to which we have been introduced by many of the speakers have been theological, philosophical, historical, socio-political, etc. The lens I use will be experiential, personal and narrative. From this perspective, we will be able to see, with the combination of the other "eyes," how one particular person has walked this journey and seen creation and the created world in ways that would never have been possible without a leap of faith. So with all of this as background and context, I will use this figurative lens to look at three distinct field experiences of my own. This lens will initially magnify the experiences; and then, by reversing the lens, we will be able to see the broader context of the very same experiences.

I would like to present my reflections on Franciscans and Creation from a perspective of inductive insights rather than the deductive insights proposed by my fellow friars in the previous presentations. I do not believe that one approach is more significant than the other. Rather, I believe that we need both ways of looking at the created world. It is not unlike the difference between seeing with binocular vision and with monocular vision. Depth perception is a way of seeing that is not possible, or at least very difficult to achieve, with monocular vision. One way of vision provides some insight, but having a second eye gives not only a second perspective but depth perception as well.

In my desire to share my Franciscan perspective to a diverse audience, I find myself dealing with an inner struggle. The insights of a Franciscan perspective are too important to leave to a single style of learning or to a single way of sensing the world. And so, I must honor both my scientist's eye and my spiritual eye. To acknowledge my social location and some of my known biases, I need to share a bit about my personal background. Prior to entering the Franciscans, I worked for nearly thirteen years in the academic world of a major land-grant university. In this world, I taught undergraduate and graduate students and did research in plant physiology. My world and life experience was that of research laboratories, graduate students, technicians and postdoctoral associates. It was as much a world of walking through corn-fields and greenhouses in the blistering summer heat of Texas as it was an air-conditioned world of laboratory research, grant writing, academic publishing and teaching. And, as much as I loved what I was doing as a researcher and teacher, I also yearned to stretch myself more and more towards the poor and powerless of the world. I yearned for a simpler lifestyle that might allow me more time to spend with God the Creator. I had no idea of how I might bring together such disparate perspectives. I did know that continuing my faith journey meant bringing together these very different worldviews.

In 1989, I began my Franciscan journey. This path and way of being slowly nurtured within me not only the language of different types of prayer but also a different way of being in this world. Bit by bit, I began to realize how my values expanded to include more of the economically and politically hidden worlds. Upon the completion of my degree in theology, my first assignment was to return to teaching biology in a Catholic university.

A New Teaching Experience

Instead of teaching third-year majors in plant sciences or graduate students as I had been doing five years earlier, I was now presented with the challenge of teaching "non-science" students, those majoring in music, business, art and humanities. Teaching students who would take their first and last science course in their lives in my classroom was a tremendous responsibility.

Within a few weeks, I realized how the more formal deductive style of lecturing would not engage these bright men and women. I quickly changed to a more inductive and experiential style of introducing the course content. I learned how to weave back and forth between inductive and deductive styles. This created an interesting dynamic tension for the students that was not only able to capture their imaginations and curiosities but provided, as well, a different context for learning some of the deductive facts and figures essential to grasping the concepts.

The great appeal of the Franciscan perspective to the general public may be because of its inductive and process-oriented style. It is by experiencing the created world, i.e. sunsets, clouds, waterfalls, birds flying overhead, that we enter into a personal relationship with nature. It was so for Francis, who was moved to write about it, e.g. the *Canticle of Creatures*. It is so for us also. Most certainly there is a philosophical, theological and scientific basis for what we see and experience. But for most of us, the initial impact is richly *sensual* rather than intellectual.

So, as I now continue with my reflection, I want to set out my greater goal–that by describing some of my experiences of nature these will help you recall some of your own. My experiences are not models nor are they normative. But they are among millions of experiences that occur to those who allow themselves to see with the eyes of a Franciscan.

Getting Your Feet Wet

Soon after I moved to Spokane, Washington, I became very aware that there was increasing public awareness of the lead pollution in the St. Joseph River that runs through Spokane on its way to form the Columbia River. Portions of the tributaries drain watershed areas that are downriver from the now inactive silver mines. These mines date back to the 1800s and were important to the economic development of the Pacific Northwest. Some five percent of the ore contained silver. Unfortunately, this same ore contained twenty-five percent lead. Over a century of active mining has resulted in dispersing lead into the Columbia River system. To learn more about the extent of the lead pollution problem, I joined an ecological in-service on lead problems in the Northwest. On this pilgrimage to different sites where the history of the Northwest was literally gouged into the natural landscape, I observed how this history had played out between two forces–human activities and nature.

Academically and intellectually, I was able to understand and appreciate the magnitude of the problem. But until I stood, in the early spring, at the confluence of two smaller tributaries, I did not appreciate the impact of this lead pollution. I could see the consequences on the riverbed vegetation. Looking at the two rivers, the contrast was dramatic. Human activities had changed the fate of all of the organisms within in these ecosystems. The issue was black and white for the naked eye to see. I did not need statistics, nor sampling strategies to see, along one of the rivers, algae growing along the bank, dead migratory birds along the water's edge, the loss of clarity in the flowing water, nor even the effect on trees and shrubs downwind from the ore processing areas. Statistical tables could never have represented more effectively the devastation of an ecosystem.

I dipped one hand into the murky water of one river and reached over and dipped my other hand into the clear water of the other river. What more did I need to convince me of the consequences of human actions over the decades? As I stood there with one foot in one river and the other foot in the other river, I could see played out the ecological consequences of the decision to mine for silver. The power of a symbolic action of lifting a handful of water and symbolically accepting responsibility for the decisions of others–both those I agree with and those I disagree with–was a moment of reconciliation within my own heart. This now became the point of integration between the ideas floating around in my head and the feelings in the darkness of my heart. A light bulb had come on!

This experience moved me to write a proposal for an educational video on lead pollution. With twenty-five thousand dollars from public monies, we mass-produced a ten-minute-video and gave it to every household on the river in the State of Washington. This single public educational video was crucial in gaining the political support of Washington residents. They challenged the EPA to recognize its responsibilities to assist more vigorously in the restoration of the largest superfund site in the Northwest.

Recycling Gone Bad

One of the most toxic parts of automobile batteries is the lead core. A common and profitable method for recycling this lead is literally to melt the lead and pour it into ingots for resale. On one of my trips to the San Diego area, one the friars asked me to join him in a visit to an abandoned auto battery recycling facility in the *maquilladoras* of Tijuana, Mexico. Batteries had been trucked there from San Diego to be melted down and recycled. A few years earlier, a fire had destroyed the entire facility. Workers in the neighboring village were very concerned about their children playing in the burned-out facility. They put barbed wire around it and painted danger signs on a cinder block wall they built beyond the fence.

As we walked around the walled structure, we could peer into the recycling areas and see the huge cauldrons that had been used to melt the lead from the discarded batteries. We could also see that the lead salts were leeching through the cinder block wall and literally dissolving it. We came upon a trench that had been dug to assess soil quality. It was eight feet long, four feet wide and seven feet deep. About three feet below the surface of the soil, there was a foot-wide white band of chemicals seeping below the ground and running the entire length of the trench. The lead was clearly seeping underground.

My mind was racing along making mental notes about the kind of proposal I would like to submit to study this site for recommendations for remediation and cleanup. I thought perhaps one hundred thousand dollars a year for three years might cover the cost. I thought of making connections with the local university or college and their chemistry or biology department. It would be good to have a graduate student work on this project. Maybe someone in analytical chemistry would find this an interesting project. We could also connect with someone from the universities in San Diego. My mind was harking back to the days when I had done this for my job.

While I was looking into the trench, a worker with his lunch pail walked past us, heading down a trail. We saw that the trail led to a small town about a thousand feet below, winding down the side of the mountain where were standing. As I looked at the rooftops and the layout of the town, I wondered what the local health workers were do-ing. Who was the community activist who knew this was happening and perhaps needed some inspiration to address this problem? Was there a public health nurse working on it. Were there any parents in those houses concerned that a strange chemical might be seeping into their valley? At the very base of the mountainside was a cornfield with stalks about two feet high.

A light bulb came on once again. The answer to this problem cer-tainly involved some technology. But more important, the answer needed the joint efforts of the people to make it happen. The human relationships in this community would be as important as having the right technology and administrative support.

These were the moments when I realized that my roles as a Franciscan and as a scientist were not incompatible but complimentary. It became clear that life's problems are not always solved by more money or more technology. Life involved not only technology but the heart as well. We need both perspectives to see the depth of God's love in our world. Each perspective is like the lens I spoke of earlier. Each lens has to be polished and used very carefully. It is possible to use just one lens at a time, but when we learn how to look through both lenses at once, we begin to see how God must see us.

Our journey as Franciscans is to search out of the darkness of our hearts. As we learn how to do this for ourselves, we can then walk with others who share this journey of faith. In the common journey we can reach out to each other and help each other as sometimes we stray from this path. And in the end, we give thanks to God for God's patience in being with us on this journey.

When the Truth Hits: the Story of Zechariah and Elizabeth

At the end of my course on Human Ecology, I tell the students I understand that for many of them this will be their last course in the sciences. I ask them to put themselves in the place of Zechariah when the Angel told him that he was to be the father of a son. As Zechariah questioned the Angel, the Angel struck Zechariah silent. For any teacher or prayer leader, being struck silent is a great loss. As you learn truth in the ecological world around you, are you silent like Zechariah? Zechariah broke his silence when his son John was being named in the temple. Seeing his son being named was the truth that he could no longer deny. What will be the moment of truth for you? For what reason will you be silent in your life about your faith? When will that light bulb come on for you? What will it take to turn that light on? Let us recall from our Franciscan tradition: "Most high glorious God, enlighten the darkness of my heart. Give me correct faith, certain hope, and perfect charity, sense and knowledge so I might always discern your holy and true will" (*Prayer Before the Crucifix*).

CHAPTER SIX

IS CREATION A WINDOW TO THE DIVINE? A BONAVENTURIAN RESPONSE

Zachary Hayes, O.F.M.

Contemporary writers about scientific issues cover a wide range of possibilities. At one end of the spectrum we find people such as Timothy Ferris and Steven Weinberg. In his book entitled *The Whole Shebang*, Ferris takes his readers through a remarkable cosmic journey, which lasts for twelve chapters, or three hundred and two pages. The book ends with something called a "Contrarian Theological Afterword." It is here that the author asks what this cosmology might tell us about God.

> Sadly, but in all earnestness, I must report that the answer as I see it is: Nothing. Cosmology presents us neither with the face of God, nor with the handwriting of God, nor such thoughts as may occupy the mind of God. This does not mean that God does not exist, or that he does not create the universe or universes. It means that cosmology offers no resolution to such questions.[1]

He then goes on to explain in more detail what he has in mind. It seems to be basically the conviction that scientific cosmology can neither prove nor disprove the existence of God. This may well be the case. But does it lead us to say that the scientific vision of cosmic reality tells us nothing about God? Might it be important to nuance this more carefully?

In one of the most provocative statements in current publications about science, Steven Weinberg, in *The First Three Minutes*, after describing the mathematical logic that seems to underlie the cosmic order and its functioning, makes the following statement: "The more the universe seems comprehensible, the more it also seems pointless."[2] And while he sees science as our most reliable path to truth, precisely as a scientist he rejects any hint that there might be purpose, design, or God behind the majestic scheme he discovers in the cosmos. So from this form of scientific reflection there is significant literature that speaks of the pointlessness of the universe, or of a universe that seems to be tragically

91

indifferent to any search for meaning. Certainly, if this were the whole of the material available today, the answer to the question in our title would seem to be an emphatic "No!"; that is, unless one chose to ignore the insights of so many outstanding scientists in favor of a medieval form of physics such as that which we clearly find in the work of St. Bonaventure and other outstanding medieval theologians.

However, at the other end of the spectrum of scientific writers are many who speak of their work as "reading the mind of God." I first noticed this phrase at the end of Stephen Hawking's *Brief History of Time*. He had just described how, sometime in the future, we will have discovered a complete theory to explain what the universe is and how it functions. Then we will be able to gather around another sort of question; namely, *Why* is it that we and the universe exist? If we find the answer to that, it would be "the ultimate triumph of human reason–for then we would know the mind of God."[3] On my bookshelf next to this slim volume of Hawking are three other books that speak of the mind of God.[4] In every case here, we have instances of scientists or writers about science reflecting on the experience of the scientist doing the work of the scientist and speaking about it in language that evokes a sense of the vision of St. Augustine, who so clearly saw the created cosmos as an external expression of the eternal Word that was immanent in the very mystery of God. How this language is to be understood in the authors mentioned remains to be seen. But at neither end of the spectrum are we dealing with conclusions based strictly on scientific method. Rather we are dealing with instances of personal or philosophical assumptions blended into the thinking of writers concerned with science. It seems that for those who take the first position, the answer to the question in the title must be a "no." And the ideas suggested in the work of Bonaventure will sound hopelessly archaic. But for those who resonate with the language at the second end of the polarity, the views of Bonaventure may be of considerable interest.

In the area of theology itself, the last few years have seen some significant publications. Langdon Gilkey, in a book entitled *Nature, Reality and the Sacred*,[5] asks in what sense, if any, nature can be seen as a reflection of the divine. There are qualities that are there for anyone to observe, but only for a person of theistic faith can they be seen as reflections of the divine. It is important from Gilkey's perspective to recognize the multi-dimensional knowledge of nature; i.e., viewing it through different "glasses" or disciplines or faith-convictions. No single one of these can legitimately claim to be the "only" legitimate way.

At quite a different level, Elizabeth Johnson gave her presidential address at the 1996 convention of the Catholic Theological Society of America. It was entitled: "Turn to the Heavens and the Earth: Retrieval of the Cosmos in Theology."[6] She treats the place that the physical universe played in the theology of the past and the obvious absence of this in more recent theology. Her concern is with the impoverishment of theology in the light of this lack, as well as with the ethical implications of this situation. And there is the outstanding work of John Haught whose books and articles are very helpful in dealing with questions about the relation between science and theology. A very recent article of his is entitled "The Unfinished Universe: Does Creation Tell a Story?"[7]

This is just a sampling of the recent material developed theologically that indicates the possible significance of a reading of Bonaventure. At quite a different level is the work of Russell Stannard, an outstanding British high-energy nuclear physicist. In a book entitled *The God Experiment*, he writes: "Accepting God as Creator of the world opens up the possibility of learning more about Him from the study of that world."[8] Stannard first appeals to the relation between an artist and the work of art; and between a woman and the fruit of her womb. He then singles out a number of specific issues from a scientific understanding of the world that might point to certain aspects of the mystery of the divine; for example, the immense size of the universe, the unimaginable reach of cosmic time, the emergence of a certain order in the context that reveals much randomness. He ends this section with the following:

> There is an orderliness to the way the world runs–it is not chaotic. It is beautiful; there is a lovely use of symmetry; there is breathtaking simplicity and economy in the basic building blocks of matter and the interactions between them–and yet these are able in ingenious ways to give rise to unlimited richness and variety. Is this not saying something about the way the mind of God works?[9]

Our approach is not to prove the existence of God from our experience of the created order. It is rather to work with the conviction that, for one who believes in God, the cosmos can open such a person to an ever deeper sense of awe at the mystery of the cosmos, which suggests dimensions of the mystery of the divine. Looking back to Bonaventure, we see one who consciously operated against the background of philosophical exemplarity. This has to do with the relation between cause and effect, or between an artist and the work of art in a way that is similar to what we have just seen in Stannard. When we turn to the work of Bonaventure with this in mind, it is interesting to see how he develops the analogy of a book, written "within" and "without." And some of his central themes are: the divine fertility, beauty, art, etc. Some examples might be helpful.

The Big Bang model of science suggests that, huge as it is, the whole of the cosmos came originally from one point. Hence, all things as we know them in this cosmos go back to a common source. Development and change (evolution) is the stuff of our history, but finally it all comes from one root foundation. It is not difficult to relate this to Bonaventure's descriptions of God as the inexhaustible source of all that is. Also, it signals an awareness of the unity and fecundity of God in Bonaventure's thought. And there is the emergence of order out of what seemed to be chaos, and the beauty of the drama of life emerging from very simple elements reaching out into the immensity of time and space. This is reminiscent of what in Bonaventure's language is called the simplicity of God and of the *plenitudo fontalis*.

Another metaphor used by both Augustine and Bonaventure describes creation as a beautiful poem or song of God.[10] The Latin word *carmen* can be translated either as poem or as melody. To get a better sense of how this metaphor works, we need to think of the structure of a melody and what makes a successful melody. A melody is not just a series of notes in juxtaposition. A well-crafted melody relates individual notes to other notes in terms of pitch and rhythm in such a way that the true significance of the individual note can be discerned only through the network of relations which make up the whole of the melody. If we think of the cosmos in terms of this metaphor, it suggests the need for a sense of wholeness, a sense of inter-relatedness of all the elements that make up the melody of the cosmos, and the hope that there is, in the context of the wild diversity of creatures, some form of unity and order. It is not difficult to relate this to what contemporary cosmology sees as systems within systems, all the way down (Quark research at Fermi Laboratory) and all the way out into space (Hubble telescope).

Bonaventure expands this in a similar way. Again, the Trinity is seen as supreme creative love and goodness, the fount from which all created reality pours forth. The divine Word in the mind of God is the perfect expression of all that God is within the Godhead and all that God can call into being in creation. As we have seen above, the metaphor of language helps develop the implications of this. We might also think of it in terms of a painting and the copies of the painting. All the copies resemble the original to some degree. We can well think of the great El Greco painting of the Blessed Virgin mounted on the wall in the Art Institute in Chicago. That is the original. There are many prints available in the gift-shop, but some of the copies are better than others. In a similar way, all creatures reflect the divine Word in some way, some more fully than others. This language-metaphor can be extended to take the form of a book. And the whole of creation can be seen as a book. The content of the book is first written in the mind of God. As we learn to read the book of creation, we come to learn something of the mind of God.

This can be related in a different way to the mystery of the Trinity, which tells us that God is through and through relational. We are not surprised, therefore, to discover the depth of inter-relatedness throughout the created cosmos.

Then there is in Bonaventure's work the analogy of the stained glass window. Here we must think of the stained glass of Notre Dame cathedral and the Sainte-Chapelle, both in Paris at the time Bonaventure used the window as a metaphor for creation. Walk into either one of these buildings on a sunny day and you are overwhelmed by the remarkable display of light and color in the glass and on the floor. This Bonaventure uses as a metaphor for creation:

> In every creature there is a shining forth of the divine light; . . .
> As you notice that a ray of light coming in through a window is
> colored according to the shades of the different panes of glass,
> so the divine light shines differently in each creature and even
> in the various properties of the creatures.[11]

As the colored patterns on the floor of the cathedral are generated by the physical light pouring through the glass, so the patterns of created things are generated by the divine creativity, which shines through differently in each individual thing and in each property of each thing. The cosmos is, as it were, a window opening to the divine. The rich variety of creatures and their specific qualities is a reflection of the depth and richness of the divine Trinity. Seeing this richness of creation as a contemporary scientist, Stephen Jay Gould names one of his books *Full House*.

To use another metaphor that points in the same direction, Bonaventure uses the phenomenon of water. The trinitarian God of productive love can be compared with a living fountain of water. Flowing from that fountain as something known, loved and willed into being by the creative love of God is the immense river of creation. The world of nature in its vastness is the expression of a loving, intelligent Creator. As a reflection of the richness of the creative source, the cosmos cannot be one-dimensional. Think of water also in the form of the ocean and it suggests the overwhelming fullness of creation as it comes from the depths of God. Like an ocean, the cosmos is deep and contains many levels of meaning. No one form of created being is an adequate expression of the immensely fertile source that resides in the divine, creative love. Therefore the diversity of beings that in fact exist is a more appropriate form of divine self-expression.

In medieval theology, the human soul of Christ is mirrored in the spiritual nature of the angels. And the whole of the visible creation is sculpted after Christ's human body. The mystery of Christ encapsulates something of all creation in itself. All the glories of nature—the heavenly galaxies, the cataracts of mountain springs, the tender flowers of springtime—all catch a gleam of Christ's beauty and embody just a spark of his charm. The beauty of the divine life embodied in Christ is refracted in countless ways in the glories of the created order. For Bonaventure, the eternal Word is the center of God's divine life. As the Word incarnate, he is the center of God's external work in creation and in history. As the "first born of all creatures," he is the center of creation. As the crucified and risen Lord, he embodies the end or purpose of creation. Rising from the dead, he anticipates what God intends for the whole of creation—to return to the depths of divine life and love from which all things came initially.

In a remarkable sermon on the mystery of the Transfiguration of Christ, Bonaventure describes it in the following words:

> All things are said to be transformed in the transfiguration of Christ, in as far as something of each creature was transfigured in Christ. For as a human being, Christ has something in common with all creatures. With the stone he shares existence; with plants he shares life; with animals he shares sensation; and with the angels he shares intelligence. Therefore, all things are said to be transformed in Christ since—in his human nature—he embraces something of every creature in himself when he is transfigured. [12]

Implications of a Bonaventurian View

1) This is a view that highlights the religious meaning of material creatures, including the human body. We can be serious about the meaning of material creation without identifying created reality with the divine. We should relate to the world of nature with gratitude, respect and with a sense of responsibility for the good of the whole.

2) It also emphasizes the religious meaning of sense experience. In all beautiful things, one can come to a sense of the divine beauty. Creation can become a means for the discovery of God. This is a spirituality that orientates the person more emphatically to the meaning of this world as God's creation and to the possibility of finding God in everyday affairs.

3) The created order can awaken us to the mystery of the richness of the divine creative love so that we can become the conscious mouthpiece of the entire cosmos, giving conscious voice to what every creature says in itself: Each creature in some way calls out "God." Human beings do that in the name of all through knowledge, consciousness and love. The Holy Father has encouraged us to come to a better understanding of the sciences. To do this does not mean that we destroy Christian faith. Quite the contrary, it can deepen our sense of awe and admiration for the mystery that is God's creation.

4) This tradition communicates a very strong sacramental sense. By sacramental we mean that the mystery of God's self-communication is mediated to us in a tangible form. If this tradition becomes our guide, it means that sacraments are not simply certain ceremonies that we enact in church. These are, indeed, sacraments. But they are embedded in a universe that as a whole is sacramental. The whole of the cosmos is a language system that mediates the mystery of God to those who learn to read it. Thus the tradition alerts us to the sacred character of the cosmos. This does not mean that we identify the universe with God. But it means that we learn to see it as a means of manifesting and communicating the divine to the human. This sense of the sacramental quality of the cosmos is radicalized in the Christian perception of Christ. The human reality of Jesus is the most focused statement of what God is about with the

world more generally. Jesus is the pre-eminent instance of the sacramentality of the cosmos.

5)   Einstein once said that one of the deepest questions raised for us by science is the following: Is the universe friendly or unfriendly? In this he suggests what seems to be the inevitable conclusion from much of science: namely, the cosmos is very ambiguous when viewed only from a scientific perspective. And many people, looking at that vision, come to a very fatalistic sense of reality. Steven Weinberg, as we have seen, once wrote: "the more intelligible it seems, the more pointless!"

This might suggest the need for the wisdom of the religious vision to bring to bear on Einstein's question. If we do this from the tradition of Christian theology, the almost fatalistic character of contemporary physics begins to take on a friendlier character. While physics properly does its job in describing the historical unfolding of cosmic reality, theology will give more emphasis to the presence of God and the divine immanence to the world in the historical unfolding described by science. I will close with a quote from Bonaventure:

> Therefore any person who is not illumined by such great splendor in created things is blind. Anyone who is not awakened by such great outcries is deaf. Anyone who is not led by such effects to give praise to God is mute. Anyone who does not turn to the First Principle as a result of such signs is a fool. Therefore open your eyes; alert your spiritual ears; unlock your lips, and apply your heart so that in all creatures you may see, hear, praise, love, and adore, magnify, and honor your God lest, the entire world rise up against you. [13]

Endnotes

[1]Timothy Ferris, *The Whole Shebang: A State-of-the-Universe(s) Report* (New York: Simon & Schuster, 1997), 303-304.

[2]Steven Weinberg, *The First Three Minutes* (New York: Basic Books, 1977), 144. Weinberg himself comments on this and on the reaction it has evoked in his later book, *Dreams of a Final Theory* (New York: Pantheon Books, 1992), 255, 313.

[3]Stephen Hawking, *A Brief History of Time: From the Big Bang to Black Holes* (New York: Bantam Books, 1988), 175.

[4]Paul Davies, *The Mind of God: The Scientific Basis for a Rational World* (New York: Simon & Schuster, 1992); James Trefil, *Reading the Mind of God: In Search of the Principle of Universality* (New York: Scribner's, 1989); Mariano Artigas, *The Mind of the Universe: Understanding Science and Religion* (Philadelphia: Templeton Foundation, 2000).

[5]Langdon Gilkey, *Nature, Reality, and the Sacred: The Nexus of Science and Religion* (Minneapolis: Fortress Press, 1993), 175ff.

[6]*Catholic Theological Society Proceedings* 52 (1996): 1-14.

[7]*Commonweal* 130.5 (March 14, 2003): 12ff.

[8]Russell Stannard, *The God Experiment: Can Science Prove the Existence of God?* (Mahwah, NJ: Hidden Spring, 1999), 193.

[9]Stannard, 194.

[10]*Breviloquium*, Prologus, #2 (V, 204).

[11]*Collationes in Hexaemeron*, 12, 14 (V, 386).

[12]*Sermo I for the second Sunday of Lent* (IX, 218).

[13]*Itinerarium Mentis in Deum* in: *Works of St. Bonaventure*, vol. 2, ed. P. Boehner, O.F.M. and Z. Hayes, O.F.M. (St. Bonaventure, NY: Franciscan Institute Publications, 2002), 61.

AUTHORS

Ilia Delio, O.S.F., a member of the Franciscan Servants of the Holy Child Jesus, North Plainfield, New Jersey, did her doctoral studies in theology at Fordham University. She is presently at Washington Theological Union, Washington, D.C., serving as Associate Professor of Ecclesial History and Franciscan Studies and as Director of the Franciscan Center. She is author of *Crucified Love: Bonaventure's Mysticism of the Crucified Christ* (Quincy: Franciscan Press, 1998), *Simply Bonaventure: An Introduction to His Life, Thought, and Writings* (New York: New City Press, 2001) and *A Franciscan View of Creation: Learning to Live in a Sacramental World*, Vol. 2, The Franciscan Heritage Series (CFIT-ESC-OFM) (St. Bonaventure, NY: Franciscan Institute Publications, 2003).

Franklin Fong, O.F.M., a friar of the St. Barbara Province, California, is a plant physiologist. He did his doctoral studies at the University of California, Riverside. He also holds a Master's degree in Theological Studies from the Franciscan School of Theology in Berkeley. Fong was an Associate Professor of Plant Physiology in the Department of Soil and Crop Sciences, Texas A & M University, before joining the friars. He also taught at Gonzaga University, Spokane, Washington. He has published widely in the areas of plant hormones and environmental physiology. For the past five years he has served as vocations director for his province.

John F. Haught did his doctoral studies at Catholic University in Washington, D.C. He is presently the Thomas Healey Distinguished Professor of Theology at Georgetown University. His area of specialization is systematic theology with a particular interest in issues pertaining to science, cosmology, ecology and religion. He has published widely. Among his works are: *Deeper than Darwin: The Prospect for Religion in the Age Of Evolution* (2003) and *God After Darwin: A Theology of Evolution* (2000), both published by Westview Press. Paulist Press has published the following works by him: *Responses to 101 Questions on God and Evolution* (2001); *Science and Religion: From Conflict to Conversation* (1995); *The Promise of Nature: Ecology and Cosmic Purpose* (1993); *What Is Reli-*

gion? (1990); *What Is God?* (1986); *The Cosmic Adventure* (1984); *Religion and Self-Acceptance* (1976). In addition to these, he is author of *Mystery and Promise: A Theology of Revelation* (Liturgical Press, 1993), *The Revelation of God in History* (Michael Glazier Press, 1988), and *Nature and Purpose* (University Press of America, 1980). He also served as editor for *Science and Religion in Search of Cosmic Purpose* (Georgetown University Press, 2000). In 1996, Haught established the Georgetown Center for the Study of Science and Religion.

Gabriele Ühlein, O.S.F., a Franciscan Sister of Wheaton, Illinois, is an author, a theologian and an artist. She received her doctoral degree in process theology from Chicago Lutheran Seminary and has worked extensively in the area of Jungian psychology. As a speaker, retreat facilitator and writer, she is well-known in the Franciscan family for her practical and spiritual perspectives. She is founder of the FranCIScan Center for Incarnation Studies–a resource center "without walls," dedicated to recovering and celebrating the spiritual legacy of Sts. Francis and Clare and based on the incarnation-oriented context of the "Canticle of the Creatures." Currently, she serves in leadership ministry–in Wheaton as a province councilor in her own international Franciscan congregation and nationally as president of the Franciscan Federation.

Keith Douglass Warner, O.F.M., is a friar of the St. Barbara Province, California. An artist and a geographer, he is a doctoral candidate in the Environmental Studies Department at the University of California, Santa Cruz. He also lectures at Santa Clara University. Warner has a Master's degree in Franciscan Spirituality from the Franciscan School of Theology in Berkeley, where he is now a regent. From 1996-99, he helped lead a popular education campaign about economic justice at the St. Anthony Foundation in San Francisco's Tenderloin neighborhood. His research interests include sustainable agriculture initiatives, water resources in the West and the interface between religious and environmental values. His dissertation analyzes the extension of agro-ecological knowledge into conventional agriculture in California. With John E. Carroll, he edited *Ecology and Religion: Scientists Speak* (Quincy, IL: Franciscan Press, 1998).

Zachary Hayes, O.F.M., is a member of the Sacred Heart Province of Friars Minor and serves as the Duns Scotus Professor of Spirituality at Catholic Theological Union in Chicago. A renowned medieval scholar and writer, Hayes received his doctor of theology degree from the University of Bonn, Germany. His extensive work on the writings of St. Bonaventure over the last thirty years has provided the foundation for a Bonaventurian revival in the English-speaking world. He has also written in the area of modern Christian thought, especially eschatology, and is currently working on problems in the area of religion and science. He is the author of numerous books and articles. His most recent books include *A Window to the Divine: A Theology of Creation* (Quincy, IL: Franciscan Press, 1997) and the *Gift of Being* (Collegeville, MN: Liturgical Press, 2001).

Dawn M. Nothwehr, O.S.F, is a Franciscan Sister of Rochester, Minnesota, and an Assistant Professor of Ethics at Catholic Theological Union in Chicago. She has a Master of Arts degree in Religious Studies from the Justice and Peace Institute of the Maryknoll School of Theology, where she specialized in feminist theology and theologies of liberation. She did her doctoral studies at Marquette University, where she was a Teaching Fellow (1993-94). She has taught theology at Quincy University, at St. Norbert College, De Pere, Wisconsin, at St. Xavier University, Chicago, and at St. Bernard's Institute, Colgate Divinity School, Rochester, New York. Her main interest is the ethics of power and the role of mutuality in the moral life. Her research is undergirded by significant experience in pastoral work with marginalized peoples, by diocesan social ministry and by the study and praxis of liberation theologies and feminist ethics. She is editor of *Franciscan Theology of the Environment: An Introductory Reader* (Quincy, IL: Franciscan Press, 2002) and author of *Mutuality: A Formal Norm for Christian Social Ethics* (San Francisco: Catholic Scholars Press, 1998), as well as numerous articles.